LISTEN TO ME

COMMUNICATING THE NEEDS OF PEOPLE WITH PROFOUND INTELLECTUAL AND MULTIPLE DISABILITIES

of related interest

Home at Last
How Two Young Women with Profound Intellectual and
Multiple Disabilities Achieved Their Own Home
Pat Fitton, Carol O'Brien and Jean Willson
Foreword by James Hogg
ISBN 1 85302 254 3

Making Music with the Young Child with Special Needs
A Guide for Parents
Elaine Streeter
ISBN 1 85302 187 3

Language Development in Children with Special Needs
Performative Communication
Irene Johansson
Translated by Eva Thomas
ISBN 1 85302 241 1

LISTEN TO ME

COMMUNICATING THE NEEDS OF PEOPLE WITH PROFOUND INTELLECTUAL AND MULTIPLE DISABILITIES

Pat Fitton

Foreword by Harry Marsh

Jessica Kingsley Publishers
London and Bristol, Pennsylvania

First published in the United Kingdom in 1994 by
Jessica Kingsley Publishers Ltd
116 Pentonville Road
London N1 9JB, England
and
1900 Frost Road, Suite 101
Bristol, PA 19007, U S A

Library of Congress Cataloging in Publication Data
Fitton, Pat, 1947–
Listen to me: communicating the needs of people with profound
and multiple disabilities / Pat Fitton
p. cm.
Includes bibliographical references and index.
ISBN 1-85302-244-6
1. Communication in services for the handicapped--Great Britain–
2. Communication in services for the handicapped--Great Britain--
Case studies. 3. Handicapped--Care--Great Britain.
4. Handicapped--Care--Great Britain--Case studies. 5. Fitton,
Kathy, d. 1991. I. Title.
HV1559.G6F57 1994
362,4'048--dc20

British Library Cataloguing in Publication Data
A CIP catalogue record for this book is available from the British Library

ISBN 1 85302 244 6

Printed and Bound in Great Britain by
Biddles Ltd, Guildford and King's Lynn

CONTENTS

For Kathy and everyone
who loved her

Acknowledgements

The following people have given generously of their time in reading my manuscript, advising and encouraging me: Professor James Hogg, Director, White Top Research Unit, University of Dundee; Ann Hunt, Family Care Officer, Tuberous Sclerosis Association; Dr. Susannah Kahtan, a director of Medical Education on Disability, University College and Middlesex School of Medicine; Harry Marsh, Director, Contact a Family; Ann Worthington, Founder/Organiser, In Touch.

My thanks to Lesley Brown, RADAR; Carers National Association; Gini Cloke, Bob Snow, SENSE, Midlands; Maria Duggan; Matthew Griffiths, Hannah Harris, Katie Rowan MENCAP; Helen Mount, Co-ordinator, PIMD Section, MENCAP; Carol O'Brien; Simon Palmour; Joan Rush, Andrea Whittaker, Kings Fund; Mark Vaughan CSIE; James Rye, Spastics Society, for their advice and help at various stages of the work.

Any remaining errors are entirely my responsibility.

Marin Battye and Liz Goldsmith gave permission for the physiotherapy diagram in Chapter 2 to be used. It is based on one in 'The caring person's guide to handling the severely miltiply handicapped', Macmillan. It was adapted by Amanda Wright, lecturer in Physiotherapy, Kings College, when she was working as a community physiotherapist with my daughter.

Special thanks to the Goldsmiths' Company who funded my secondment to do the writing, to the Headteacher and Governors of Northumberland Park Community School who agreed to my leave of absence, and to my colleagues who took on extra work as a result.

Lastly and above all, to my husband Barrie and my friends Alyson Ruddock and Jean Willson, whose own experiences have enriched my work, and whose unlimited love and support have enabled me to complete this book and to find some purpose in life after Kathy.

THIS BOOK IS NOT

A complete guide to caring for and supporting people with profound intellectual and multiple disabilities, nor is it a compendium of information about services.

THIS BOOK IS

An affirmation of the right of people with profound intellectual and multiple disabilities, and their carers, to lead a full and meaningful life.

It offers some practical ideas for making this possible, with special emphasis on communicating the rights and needs of the person you care for. It focuses on those whose degree of learning disability makes it impossible for them to do this themselves. It concentrates on what needs to be done and gives advice on how to go about it.

ON USING THIS BOOK

Each chapter deals with communicating these rights and needs in a particular situation. At the end of each chapter there is a list of references for further information or reading. My daughter appears throughout the book as a practical example or illustration in many of the situations.

While I was writing this book there were many changes in laws and government policies in education, community care and benefits. Organisations changed their addresses, and individuals within them came and went. I have updated all information and references as new details came in.

The problems, issues and principles in the book remain the same even if in future some details may change. However, when taking action, you should always check that you have up-to-date details and further information on the laws and rules that apply, using the references given in the book.

When organisations change address, you can find the new details by contacting the national MENCAP information section, telephone number 071–454–0454.

This book is written from twenty-seven years' experience of loving and caring and fighting, for and alongside my daughter. Kathy died in August 1991 and this book offers some of that experience to help others like her and us.

This Book is For...

This book is first of all for people with profound intellectual and multiple disabilities, even though they will never read it.

This book is secondly for parents, families and carers of people with profound intellectual and multiple disabilities. It is meant to be of practical help in establishing the needs and rights of the person you care for and in communicating those needs to other people who will make decisions about them. It offers some practical suggestions about making life more interesting and worthwhile for the person with the disability and those around them.

This book is also for doctors, nurses, teachers, voluntary workers, social workers, physiotherapists, local authority officials, health service planners, and all other members of the caring professions who deal directly with or make decisions about people with disabilities. I hope it will give them insight into the pressures and dilemmas facing people with disabilities and their carers.

I want this book also to be for local councillors, members of parliament and government ministers, and others who have such power over the lives of people with disabilities.

This book may also be of use to those who care for other groups of people with special needs such as elderly frail people or children and adults who have chronic or terminal illness. Some of the practical ideas may help, and many of the general principles are similar, especially the key one, which is to see the person first, before the disability or illness.

FOREWORD

Listen to Me deserves a wide readership for several reasons. First, because it provides a means of greater understanding of people who have multiple and severe disabilities. Second, it reveals the critically important and demanding roles played by parents and other carers. Pat Fitton tells us that the book is not intended to be a complete guide. Nevertheless, I feel that she has provided in *Listen to Me* advice and information of considerable breadth and depth. The book is, I believe, modern in concept and in its argument. The emphasis throughout is on the needs and rights of the disabled person and her family.

The majority of parents and carers of people with disabilities have a very hard time in obtaining vital information. Fragmented or poorly organised services, rapid staff turnover, rigid professional practices and personalities can all present major obstacles to good quality care for disabled people, and to the recognition of the importance of parents and others as carers. Pat Fitton gives us a thoughtful and clear account of what is demanded of the parent and carer, and also of what they might reasonably expect our education, welfare benefits, health, leisure and social services to provide when someone has a disability.

The subject headings of the book come to life through the author's relationship with her daughter, Kathy. For me, this made *Listen to Me* very moving and very informative at the same time: it is difficult to recall many books which have such a powerful effect.

There has been some research undertaken in recent years which has sought to establish the types of support which parents and carers have found helpful. An important source of support mentioned by many parents is the information, advice and empathy received from other parents and carers. *Listen to Me* is a major contribution to that tradition of mutual support and understanding. I share the author's view that it behoves our legislators, policy makers and professional practitioners to smooth the path of the person with disabilities and her carers, rather than to put obstacles in their way.

Harry Marsh,
Director, Contact a Family

KATHY

If we were telling a doctor about Kathy, it sounded like this.

Kathy has cerebral palsy with severe learning difficulties. She developed rheumatoid arthritis at the age of four years. She started having grand mal fits at the age of nine years, and her epilepsy became more severe and complex as the years went by. During her teens she developed a severe bowel disorder, later diagnosed as collagenous colitis. She had vitiligo, a condition where her skin had some patches with deepened pigment and other areas where the pigment had disappeared. Kathy could not speak, walk or see to her own personal care needs. From 1984 she had a naso-gastric tube for medication and fluids, and feeding when she was too ill to eat. Her spine became twisted and she became likely to develop severe chest infections. She had severe pain at times, and was often uncomfortable.

When we told friends and family about Kathy, it went like this.

Kathy has a strong personality, she knows what she wants and works hard to get you to understand. She loves music, from Renaissance and medieval through many classical composers, and on to most folk music and jazz; when she enjoys the music she laughs and claps – when she wants you to change the tape she groans and leans until you get the message. She loves to travel – in vehicles, on trains, on ferries. She likes long walks in her wheelchair, whether in busy city streets, country lanes, coastal paths or mountain tracks. She likes to crawl over the floor, examining people's bags and briefcases, shoes and feet. She loves fluffy jumpers and bright clothes, admiring herself in the mirror. She riffles through clothes racks in stores, shouting with delight and tugging when she likes something; we hope they don't notice the dribble. She loves to have her hair cut by her friend Alyson, and gazes at the result in the mirror. She frightened an Australian tourist in Covent Garden because she was fascinated by his hairy legs protruding from short shorts, conveniently within reach from her wheelchair, and grasped one thigh firmly. She loves food, and has gradually learned that in restaurants you look at a card for a while, then talk to someone, and then the food arrives later. When she was younger, she expected food to be on the table the minute you walked through the door, and this caused a great deal of misunderstanding. When the food arrives she claps the waiters. If it is a long time coming, she might try to intercept a passing tray, assuming it is her meal. She has some very special toys, dolls and books, and only these will do on some occasions. Kathy loves baths and swimming pools, and with her armbands she will happily splash in very deep water, enjoying watching the other swimmers. As Kathy has got older, she has become more patient with our difficulties in communicating with her. She is a lot of work but she lights up our life, always welcoming us with a smile and one of her happy sounds. She has a remarkable ability to draw love and respect from those who know and care for her.

People like Kathy deserve the very best that our society can give. They have already experienced pain and frustration to a degree that most of us will never approach. Unfortunately, their rights are often in doubt; meeting their needs adequately, a constant struggle. They, their families and carers bear a heavy burden. Communicating Kathy's needs adequately made it more likely that they would be met. This book is written to help parents and carers to understand how to communicate those needs more effectively.

Part One

Learn About Me

CHAPTER 1

DIAGNOSIS AND FIRST CONTACT WITH A HOSPITAL

People with disabilities and their carers learn about the conditions affecting them at a variety of stages. It is sometimes apparent at birth that there is a suspected disability or medical condition. The baby may be born prematurely and after treatment, perhaps in a special care baby unit, may show signs of disability. In other cases the baby appears to have no problems at birth; difficulties appear at a later stage, perhaps when the usual milestones such as sitting and standing are not reached, or when epileptic fits begin, or when the baby or toddler appears not to hear or see well, or simply the baby does not thrive and tests reveal there is a disability or medical problem. Some people become disabled at a later stage, perhaps as a result of a viral illness, an accident or a stroke. Some disabled people develop further complications or conditions later on.

How this news is given is in itself the subject for a book. There are countless stories of a diagnosis being given suddenly, in medical jargon, or in brutal terms such as 'she will never do anything for herself'. Parents are told without the partner present, or on a busy ward; they may feel they are to blame in some way, or get the impression that they or their child are not valued. It is not easy to give bad news, and the recipient may resent receiving it, however carefully it is delivered. However, there are too many parents who have experienced this, and enough research documenting the problem, for doctors not to be aware of it. It should be apparent that the shock of receiving such news may mean the parent or carer does not fully take in all the information, and it may have to be given again, several times, at later stages. As a parent, you might be upset that a positive cause has been identified, say a genetic defect, because this may have implications for any other children and for their future children. You may be equally upset that no cause has been found because you are left feeling that it is a cruel fate and that there is no meaning in life. You may realise some of the implications for everyone concerned straight away, or these may only gradually become clear to you over the next months or years.

I have talked to many parents, who have received the news about their child in many different circumstances. We have discussed what is the most difficult to cope with: knowing there are disabilities at birth; learning later, after you realise something is wrong; or having a 'normal' child who develops a viral illness or has a road traffic accident, and as a result becomes disabled. The way in which parents are told, where the situation is apparent immediately after the birth, must influence how well the baby is accepted. Those of us who learned at a later stage of the disabilities had at least built up a relationship with our child and were less likely to reject them. It is a very individual matter, – too important to be left to the chance sensitivities of individual doctors.

It is not always clear in the initial stages of investigation and diagnosis whether there is a learning disability in addition to physical disabilities. This book is about people with profound intellectual and multiple disabilities, and this combination is the most difficult to deal with. It is difficult for the disabled person to deal with, because they will not understand fully (or sometimes even at all) explanations of what is happening to them. A baby with a severe learning disability will find the world a frightening place, and will be frustrated in her efforts to understand it and communicate her needs. The disabled baby or toddler may experience pain and discomfort, and be unable to communicate the site and intensity of this. They may have feeding difficulties, and require complex medication and procedures. Communication may be very difficult to establish. Kathy lay still for the first year of her life, apparently unresponsive to looks, words and cuddles; she then screamed for the next three, making no eye contact and pushing away any bodily contact. No one can say for certain what the degree of learning difficulty is for two or three years, and no one wants to make judgements which may affect that child for life at too early a stage. However, during that uncertain period valuable time is slipping away. If parents and carers and the doctors who advise them can develop a clearer idea of the capabilities of the disabled person, they can start to take an active role in activities which will help development. A toddler with cerebral palsy, for example, who also has a severe learning disability, will require a different approach from one whose intelligence is not impaired.

How do you tell? If you talk to parents and carers of disabled children whose intelligence is not impaired, there are a thousand and one clues they find. At first these clues appear in the daily interactions of caring and play: how the child goes about solving problems and develops ways of communicating, despite deafness or an inability to articulate clearly. To notice these clues you need to value that person, and find ways of convincing those professionals who deal with the child, because decisions about future education will depend on this.

Does it matter? Surely I have been arguing that every person however severely disabled, has equal value? It matters because the disabled child with a learning difficulty will have to work much harder to understand the world and to deal with their other disabilities. It matters because anyone who cares for someone with severe disabilities, works very hard. When you are exhausted from giving twenty-four hour care, sleepless nights, apparently endless screaming and endless washing, it can tip the balance as to whether you continue if your child seems to give you no recognition, cannot receive or return affection and does not seem to be able to communicate. It matters because other people in the family, especially partners and brothers and sisters, will have their lives changed after the arrival of the disabled person, and if they are to develop a positive relationship with that person they must be able to understand what they are experiencing if they are going to make the effort to communicate.

In very practical terms, someone at this level of learning disability will eventually learn, however slowly, that 'no' means 'no'; but they may never understand why. They may try the activity again when there is nobody present to say 'no' – poking electrical sockets, eating harmful substances, or pulling the cat or dog about. Unlike infants who gradually develop the concept of danger as they grow older, people with profound intellectual and multiple disabilities may never develop this general concept.

During the 1960s it was still assumed that a child with profound intellectual and multiple disabilities would pass into institutional care, if not at first, at some point. Respite care was not easily available and families got into the sort of exhausting situation referred to above and then there only seemed one way out. Now the reverse is true, and institutional care is not considered an option for such children. However, respite care is still not easily available and crisis management still seems to rule rather than planned care. The families and carers are now expected to bear the burden and what little help is available seems to stop once school leaving age is reached. I shall deal with this issue in more detail in Chapters 10 and 11.

Now the disabled person and their carers enter a new world. They are very likely to attend outpatients' sessions at the hospital for regular check ups. They may see a number of different specialist doctors depending on the nature of the disabilities. There may be regular tests of blood and urine, other tests, some invasive and painful. There are physiotherapists, occupational therapists and orthopaedic technicians to meet. Boots, braces, splints and wheelchairs may be needed. Regular trips to hospital may be expensive and there may be problems with the care of other children at these times. Travelling may be difficult. I found that even when Kathy was small and many other parents were carrying babies and toddlers of a similar size on buses and trains, the journey was still more exhausting. Her behaviour was unpredictable, and she might scream for long periods or grab at people and their possessions. She hated sitting in a pushchair and would try to arch or slide out of it, sometimes succeeding just as we got to a kerb. She did not eat and especially drink easily, so giving her food away from home was traumatic.

This new world includes getting to know the services and benefits you need, and I shall talk about this in Chapters 13, 14 and 15. This should not be a hit or miss affair, having to find things out by chance – but it often is. These later chapters should help you to see what is available, and how to go about obtaining what is needed quickly.

If someone could have told me when Kathy was very young that some things would get easier, I may not have believed them. But they did. Perhaps parents and carers have to learn to some extent through their own experience, but others in a similar position can sometimes help them to some short cuts. First, I was trapped in the web of exhaustion that seemed to rule our life. It was hard to feel positive or even think straight in that condition. Other people in the family inevitably took second place. Second, although we seemed to spend a lot of time in clinics and hospitals, I did not feel that I was getting very helpful advice. I read books and tried to do things to help Kathy develop. I got it wrong sometimes leaving us both angry and frustrated. Third, I was beginning to lose all confidence in dealing with Kathy or anybody or anything. Fourth, Kathy and I did not seem to have a relationship; I felt great love for her but I was not getting any of the normal responses that you get from a baby. This and the exhausting round of care sometimes made me very angry, sometimes at her.

Perhaps if I describe my gradual realisation of the extent of her disabilities, it may help others going through the same experience, and may even help to get through this stage more quickly. Kathy was born a little earlier than expected, but not much. She weighed a little less than normal, but not much. She had difficulties in sucking, but not for long, although she had to go straight onto a bottle. She did not cry very much and had to be woken for night feeds as she was on the small side. She lay very quietly, and was unresponsive to physical or verbal contact. She did not make eye contact. Physically, she began to put on weight and look well. I took her to the GP and eventually to the local hospital when she had not sat up at eight months. I was told I was over-anxious and given an appointment for two months' time. The same thing happened again. When Kathy was just over a year old, she did finally sit up, although she did not seem to be doing much else. Then it was as if an explosion had taken place in our lives. She seemed suddenly to see the world for the first time, and it caused her great distress. She screamed for hours at a time, so loudly that people knocked on the front door of the house to ask if anything was wrong, for so long that I have fallen asleep and woken again to find her still screaming. I had to pad her cot to stop her hurting herself as she banged her head backwards and forwards, and her limbs against the sides. During this period, until she was two and a half years old, I was told on my regular visits to the hospital that she was 'a little bit backward'. She did not have an EEG (an examination which gives information about the brain waves) until then. The medical technician who did the test told me that it showed Kathy had severe brain damage, and signs of epilepsy, even though at that stage she had no fits. That was more than I was told when I went back to the outpatients clinic for a follow-up appointment. There was no discussion of the implications of this information, and no practical advice. I transferred Kathy to a children's hospital, and began the long journey to understanding her and helping her to make the most of her life.

Would it have helped to have had more precise information earlier? I think it is always better to know the truth. I think because Kathy looked 'normal' at that stage (despite having cerebral palsy – no doctor noticed the signs of that) assumptions were made about the reasons for her 'backward-ness' and the appropriate tests were not carried out early on. I was trying to rush her into, for example, talking, when she was still trying to cope with noticing the world around her. Once I had a clearer idea about the extent of her disabilities, although life went on being exhausting, I was able to try more concrete approaches to developing Kathy's abilities, and to appreciate each tiny bit of progress. For example, I reorganised my whole approach to mealtimes. I was determined that we would all eat together as a family, but I began to see that a table full of food and choices was confusing Kathy. It was easier for her if food was served away from the table and in separate courses. She slowly began to concentrate on her own plate instead of the other confusing bowls and dishes. It was many years before she stopped reaching out for other people's food, or pulling at the cloth to get at something tempting. I started by sitting her well out of reach of others at the table, and we stopped using tablecloths. Over a period of time she was able to accept being told not to grab other people's food, and we were eventually able to reintroduce tablecloths. Much later I realised that as she gradually understood the systems – food takes time to get cooked, the clues like the table being laid do not mean the food will arrive immediately but it will arrive, each person has their own plate, if you pull the cloth the meals will fall on the floor, when you have finished you just have to push your plate a little away, not throw it off the table – she was able to accept the rules. However, this realisation took many years, and in the meantime we had to risk the mess and disruption in order to give her the experiences to learn.

When her brother was more clear about the nature of her disability, he found it easier to accept the frustrations of living with someone who pulls your lego models apart, demolishes a shelf of goods in the supermarket and makes strange noises in the street. He played with her very naturally, which helped her development enormously, but when things went wrong he now had an explanation instead of feeling she was wilfully destructive. He felt able to explain to his friends and was happier about them coming to the house. He began to take pleasure in her progress, especially when he seemed to have a hand in it.

Could the doctors have been more helpful in this process? We eventually got a clear picture about Kathy's limitations, although the cause remained a mystery. Years later I knew better what questions to ask – is there a learning problem, is there brain damage, how severe, what information have you got from the tests, are there any other tests you could do, what other implications might there be, for example for her physical condition, and so on. I also learned to make a list of my questions before each outpatients appointment and to check them off as I asked them, making a note of any new information. I learned that there were many different kinds of doctor, and I needed to know whether I was seeing a paediatrician, who specialised in children generally, or a neurologist, a rheumatologist, a psychologist, or whatever. There seemed to be some unwritten rules to all this which I gradually picked up. It was not helpful when I turned up to an outpatients clinic and saw a different doctor from usual. I realised that the more junior doctors had to gain experience, but they seemed so rushed that they had barely had time to look at the notes, so you ended up giving a lengthy account again. I learned to make a note of what had been said and decided at the last consultation, so that I could remind an unfamiliar doctor. Sometimes the notes were missing, and sometimes they were not in order, so that it was not easy to find test results. The notes and records are so important that it must be essential to find a more efficient way of managing them. I still found doctors, even psychologists, very vague about what exactly I could do to help Kathy to learn. I was often told, 'You know her best'. This was true but not helpful. It seemed to be a long process of trial and error.

What did become clear was that Kathy must have all the normal experiences of life. She was not apparently going to learn easily the things that came to most children naturally, so she needed the experiences even more, and help to make sense of them. We went around the London parks and playgrounds, we travelled on the bus and tube, we went for day trips to the country and the seaside, we visited friends and had friends visit us, we went up to the West End and went round the stores, we went to cafes and restaurants. I was determined that Kathy would be as well dressed as any other little girl. None of this was easy. On trips out I carried a bag full of spare clothes and nappies, as Kathy ate messily and dribbled copiously, and did not use the toilet. She was small for her age, but still heavy to lift. We were managing with a large pushchair as we had not been offered a wheelchair, but humping this around and her and her supplies was tiring. Kathy still screamed a lot, especially in confined spaces, or if she had to wait for a bus or the tube. She shouted and made sounds, and grabbed at people and their possessions. We faced open prejudice, heard her called cruel names and watched other children and their parents move away from us in playgrounds. We also met people who treated her as a valid person, and we had good friends and neighbours who coped with the mess and noise she generated and made us welcome. Slowly, very slowly, she began to look at people and to make more sense of things. She learned to feed herself. At four and a half, she began to take her first steps, holding on to the furniture or our hands. Then she became very ill with a high fever. She appeared to be in terrible pain. She stopped eating and drinking. She was like this for three months, before she was diagnosed as suffering from rheumatoid arthritis. Just as we were all beginning to find our way around our new world, we were plunged into the confusion of a further dimension to our lives. I shall return to this issue in Chapter 19.

CONFIDENCE AND POWER

As we all struggled through these first miserable years, I began to realise that I was being driven along by events and the relentless daily routine. It became clear that, unless I began to take control, I would go under, and then we would collapse as a family. I have described earlier in this chapter how I gradually got the confidence to take some control of Kathy's learning. Now

I began to learn that there were rights and provisions for people like Kathy, which would help her and us to make the best we could of life. I gradually began to find out what these were, and then had to learn that it was not always a simple matter to obtain them. I had to learn the techniques of applying for all these things and then find the energy to chase and follow up and, if necessary, agitate to ensure we got them. Over the years we got help from some of the professional workers in contact with us, but our best help always came from friends with similar problems and organisations of parents and carers. Sometimes we joined with other families in organising pressure groups and action to improve facilities, both at local and national level. The rest of the book passes on what we learned together.

FURTHER INFORMATION

One important thing you need at this stage is very practical advice about things like feeding difficulties, sleeping problems, mobility, play, incontinence, coping with other children, and generally managing at home. Some organisations which help parents to get in touch with others who are dealing with similar problems are:

> Contact a Family, 170 Tottenham Court Road, London W1P 0HA. Tel: 071–383–3555. Contactline for information and advice.

> In Touch: Mrs Ann Worthington, MBE, 10 Norman Road, Sale, Cheshire, M33 3DF. Tel: 061–905–2440.

> Kith And Kids, The Irish Centre, Pretoria Road, Tottenham, London N17 8DX. Tel: 081–801–7432.

Parents and carers should know that health authorities and local authorities must provide information on all local services, including voluntary and support groups which may help you and your child. Ask your GP, consultant or social worker if you have not been given this information.

Part Two

Tell Them About Me

CHAPTER 2

WE NEED TO COMMUNICATE

Any disability involves a struggle for the disabled person and those close to them. Anyone with multiple disabilities finds that struggle a thousand times more difficult. Often one disability intensifies the effect of another. A learning disability in addition can complicate other disabilities. If compounded with severe and complex epilepsy, learning anything can be slow and frustrating, and learning some things impossible. If chronic illness is present, coping with all this is exhausting and debilitating, for the person and their carers.

In the struggle for communication with others, what do you need to say? Who do you need to tell? How much detail should you include? What different circumstances will you operate in? Most important, why do you need to say things?

WHY?

You will be doing this because the person you care for cannot do it herself. In addition to her physical disabilities she may have a significant learning disability. Her ability to understand and communicate will develop, but very slowly. She may have limited speech and/or signing; she may not speak at all. Kathy communicated with us by eye contact and a facial language of frowns, bad looks, smiles and raised eyebrows. She had a range of angry, unhappy and joyful sounds. She leaned towards objects and activities she wanted, or reached over in the desired direction. She threw objects towards one that was out of reach, to show us she wanted us to fetch it; it took us years to realise that this was communication, not being awkward. She pushed her hand towards things she wanted at table, and swept out of the way things she did not want. She did have some words by the time she was four years old, but long periods of illness and hospitalisation caused her to lose some of her skills, and the words went; only 'mama' remained. By the time, many years later, she was offered a structured approach to communication in school through a picture system, she was not willing to make the effort. She contemptuously pushed aside the pictures of, say, a meal, knowing perfectly well from sounds, sight and smells that a meal was being prepared, and unwilling to engage in what seemed to her the meaningless act of pointing to a picture of a dinner before we set hers on the table. The limitations of her system were that she could not communicate all her wishes easily, nor her more subtle feelings.

A new friend visiting us told us that Kathy was the first person with severe disabilities she had ever met. Within a very short time they were communicating very effectively. Our friend said she soon realised that Kathy 'talked' with her eyes and in other ways. Was she especially sensitive, or did she just make the effort? She went on to do music therapy with people with multiple and learning disabilities, outstanding in her ability to communicate successfully with people no one else expected to respond.

It is important to develop speech and signing with disabled people who can manage it. My experience with Kathy suggests that this needs to be managed in a structured way from as early an age as possible, otherwise the older person with an established informal system of communication may not see the point of it. There will always be some people who, because of the particular nature of their disabilities, will be unable to use speech or signing, or even gestures. Sensitivity to the 'language of the eyes' and slight movements or sounds is the key to building communication. People with severe disabilities go on trying to communicate in the face of constant frustration, misunderstanding and ignorance. We often felt clumsy and inadequate in interpreting Kathy's needs, but we got better at it over the years.

Kathy knew many of the basic things she needed to be done to keep her safe and comfortable, although with only some of these could she indicate clearly what she wanted or needed. She did not have the concept or knowledge of the wider support system she needed to survive. She did not know how we decided on and obtained her medication and other supplies. She did not know what arrangements we had to make if we were concerned about her health. She had no idea of the complex arrangements needed if we were not caring for her directly for a period. She never knew how many letters we wrote, telephone calls we made or meetings we attended to make arrangements for all her many needs. She never learned for herself such basic concepts as danger and could never be left alone, for example, with hot drinks on a table. We had to interpret her basic wishes and needs and act accordingly, and we had to learn what needed to be done about her more complex needs.

WHAT?

You will often be asked for basic details such as pregnancy and birth history, the nature and degree of disability, illness and medication, level of communication, special requirements , for example, diet, equipment, likes and dislikes, doctors involved, and so on.

WHO?

You will be telling this to your GP, consultant, nurses, ambulance workers, physiotherapists, occupational therapists, dieticians, nursery nurses, teachers, college and day centre staff, care and support workers, social workers, family, friends, voluntary workers and so on.

HOW MUCH?

You will need full details, especially of things like medication, for most professionals. You can summarise for some who are dealing with a particular aspect, such as an occupational therapist. Always include the personal aspects, whoever you are talking to. Never let anyone be dealt with as though they are just parts of the body or a medical problem.

CIRCUMSTANCES

These will include the GP's surgery, the consultant's room, the accident and emergency department, your own home, the nursery, school, college, respite care unit, other carers' homes or establishments, residential units, hospital wards, shops, restaurants, the street, parks, swimming pools, ferries, planes, other people's homes. You may be angry, frightened, anxious, depressed, calm, cheerful, harassed.

OVER AND OVER AGAIN

You will have to tell people these things over and over again. You have to tell some individuals the same thing many times. You might have to tell your life history to someone you only meet once.

The person with profound intellectual and multiple disabilities has a great need to communicate her needs. You need to be able to interpret and communicate on her behalf. You need to do this well and effectively. The rest of this book offers help in doing this.

FURTHER INFORMATION

Signing and Communication Systems

Bliss Symbolics, Thomas House, South Glamorgan Institute of Higher
    Education, Cyncoed Centre, Cyncoed Road, Cardiff CF2 6YD.
    Tel: O222–757826.

Makaton, 31 Firwood Drive, Camberley, Surrey GU15 3QD.
    Tel: 0276–61390.

Paget Gorman, 3 Gipsy Lane, Headington, Oxon OX3 7PT. Tel: 0865–61908.

Communication systems for people with sensory disabilities

Blind, Royal National Institute for the, 224, Great Portland Street, London
    W1N 6AA. Tel: 071–388–1266.

Deaf, Royal National Institute for the, 105 Gower Street, London WC1E 6AH.
    Tel: 071–387–8033.

SENSE (National Deaf-Blind and Rubella Association), 11–13 Clifton Terrace,
    Finsbury Park, London N4 3SR. Tel: 071–272–7774.

CHAPTER 3

WRITING TO PEOPLE

If in doubt, write something down. You may be confirming a telephone conversation, asking for information, requesting help, complaining or informing. If it is in writing, there is a record.

Always date letters. Always keep a copy. Letters do not have to be typed but if you are writing by hand, write with a black pen to make photo-copying easier.

Keep a note of all names, addresses, telephone numbers and their extensions, of people you are dealing with. You do not need a complicated filing system, but do keep correspondence in some sort of order so you can find things quickly. Plastic wallets for each topic – for example, benefits, wheelchair – can be kept in a box or drawer.

Keep letters short. Stick to the facts you need to present. If there are two or more topics, write separate letters for each. Busy people do not always take notice of the second point you are making.

Be straightforward, blunt if necessary. Be graphic about the way you and the disabled person are affected by the situation. Do not be embarrassed by the subject matter, for example when requesting incontinence supplies. Do not hesitate to send copies to others you may want to take an interest. If you do this, write a short covering note to them personally; they may put pressure on the person you are dealing with to sort the matter out. Build into your letter a request for a reply and specific action required. Many organisations operate on at least a fortnight's turn-round for receipt of letters, dealing with the matter and replying. If you have not heard after two weeks, write again asking for your previous letter to be dealt with.

If you meet with repeated delays and/or gross inefficiency, ask your social worker to deal with the matter. If you have not got one, or they are the cause of the delay or are the inefficient one, use a voluntary organisation, your local councillor or MP. MENCAP, the Spastics Society and many other voluntary organisations have both local and national offices, help lines and information services. You will find details at the end of Chapter 5, '*Talking to People*'.

The example below gives a frank outline of the problems leading to the request, asks for a commitment to a reply and backs up the argument with a recent recommendation from a medical body:

Mrs B. Smith,
Continence Adviser,
Midtown Borough Council.

Dear Mrs Smith,

Katherine Sirockin: Incontinence Requirements

We have sufficient Cosifit supplies for Katherine for the next two months, but I thought I would write to you now to ask for a more suitable all-in-one nappy for her in future.

Kathy still gets severe diarrhoea from her bowel disease. However, she is much better in herself due to her medication and she has a good appetite. Since she has had her naso-gastric tube, her weight has improved from 18 to 22 kilos.

As a result there are more leakages, and we can only just fasten them around her middle! Her legs have started to mark and chafe.

I enclose a leaflet about the Slipad, an all-in-one pad designed for older people with incontinence. We have tried a sample of the Model 1, which is just the right size for Kathy. The pad is more absorbent than the baby/toddler versions, but more important, the top portion is stronger with two sets of fastening tabs, so you can adjust it to a snug fit.

It goes without saying that unless we have reliable incontinence protection for Kathy, I not only have a great deal of washing of bed linen but also of her clothes, my clothes, and those of anyone else who might pick her up, furnishings and floor coverings, wheelchair cover, and so forth. Visiting friends and relatives outside the home can be embarrassing without reliable protection.

We have Kathy home every weekend and for substantial parts of the school holiday. She uses about six pads per day.

I would be grateful to know if it will be possible for the next order for Kathy's pads to be the Slipad Model 1. We shall need further supplies by early September.

I noticed that a recent report on disability from the Royal College of Physicians drew attention to the need for good assessment and provision of incontinence needs to avoid the condition further restricting the life of the sufferer.

I look forward to hearing from you,

Yours sincerely,

Some of the common difficulties we experienced in correspondence were as follows:

1. You get no reply. This happens so frequently, from local council or health authority level to government bodies, that it often seems to be a deliberate tactic rather than plain inefficiency! That is why you need a copy. After a fortnight, send a copy of the first letter with a short covering letter. Do it again if necessary.

2. You get a reply saying the matter has been passed on to someone else, who then never replies. Write back after a fortnight to the original person, asking them to ensure some action.

3. You get a reply that only partially answers your request. Write back pointing this out and repeat the points you still want help on.

4. You get a brush-off or refusal. Seek further advice from friends, professionals or the organisations referred to earlier. Do not be worried if you have been quoted official or legal jargon. We found officials often got it wrong, and sometimes seemed deliberately to mislead us.

5. Officials are interpreting policy and legal requirements in their own way. At local level, for example social services, get in touch with your ward councillor or the Chair of Social Services. At national level, contact your MP.

This is all a lot of work. Parents and carers get very tired of having to do all this as well as care for someone with complex needs. We found we still had to do it, or life was even harder because Kathy did not have what she needed.

FURTHER INFORMATION

120 Letters That Get Results. Published by the Consumers' Association (Which?); Castlemead; Gascoyne Way, Hertford, X, SG14 ILH. Tel: 0992–589031.

CHAPTER 4

Telephoning

If you do not have your own phone it can be a nightmare trying to sort things out. If you are caring for someone with profound intellectual and multiple disabilities you are entitled to have a telephone installed free of charge and to have the rental paid. You only have to pay for calls. Ask for an assessment under the Chronically Sick and Disabled Persons' Act 1970. If you have a social worker they will apply for you. If not, contact your nearest Social Services office. Keep copies of any forms you fill in or correspondence, and note the names of those who are dealing with the matter.

You will need the telephone so that you are able to contact medical and emergency services immediately you need to. You will also be able to deal with all the various people and agencies over benefits, wheelchairs, and so forth more efficiently, and without having to disrupt the routine of the person you care for.

Whenever you telephone about a matter, ask for the name of the person you are dealing with, and the extension. Always keep a pen and notepad by the phone. Make a note of all the telephone numbers you use, and all extensions and names. Keep these details in one place such as a small address book. You may need to take it out with you at times. You often get a quicker response if you are able to ask for someone by name, or refer to having spoken to a named person when discussing a matter. Examples could include: 'May I speak to Costas Demetriou in Housing Repairs Section?' or: 'I spoke to Linda Okoro yesterday about having a telephone installed, and she said I should get in touch with you.'

If someone is unhelpful or rude on the telephone, do not get drawn into an argument or allow yourself to get upset or emotional. You may feel very angry and/or may be tearful, but keep calm and look for a way forward. You could ask to speak to the person's superior, or could ring off and call back, asking to speak to someone else. If you still get nowhere, ask your social worker or a friend or a voluntary organisation to call for you. Make a note of any bad experiences and complain in writing. You are the one doing the caring and experiencing the stress and anxiety. Many professionals find their jobs stressful but it is their job – they get paid and they finish at some point. You will be caring and worrying round the clock. You may not always get the answer you want but you are entitled to receive advice and be given information in a courteous manner.

Professionals should never be surprised if carers blow their top at times. That day you may have had to deal with epileptic fits, started to wash soiled bed linen when the washing machine started leaking, received by post an unsatisfactory Statement of Special Educational Needs which is going to cause you more work to fight, had a call from school to say your child bit the escort on the bus and had your favourite plant pot pulled off the stand and smashed. Professionals should have the experience, training and good sense to deal with you sympathetically without being patronising. The exceptions need to learn that they relieve their own stress elsewhere, not on you.

FURTHER INFORMATION

If you need telephone numbers of organisations, contact the Information Section at the national MENCAP office, 071–454–0454. They have information on computer about organisations to do with all aspects of disability.

CHAPTER 5

TALKING TO PEOPLE

There is more detail about speaking to medical and similar professionals in Part Five, Doctors and Hospitals. Some general points are made here:

1. Prepare what you have to say before you meet anyone. Make brief notes, a list of questions. Consider how much detail you need to give and how far you need to summarise. Decide what the main issues are. Decide what you want to get out of the discussion and check before you go whether you have achieved this. If you have not, try to get it clear what you do next before you leave. You might, for example, have asked to meet the senior physiotherapist to request an extra session, and also to ask for support with your request for a different type of wheelchair. Ask for a reason if you are refused.

2. Do not be deflected from your purpose. If you think you are being flannelled, say so and ask to return to the point. Your written notes/questions are useful to help you bring the conversation back to its purpose. If the person you are talking to cannot resolve the matter, ask to speak to someone else. If you cannot see someone else immediately, try and arrange a further appointment before you leave.

    If you get angry or upset, ask for time to compose yourself; ask for a drink if it will help. Try to avoid walking out, however angry or frustrated you become. If you do feel obliged to walk out, be sure to follow the matter up as soon as you feel calmer.

3. Take someone with you – a partner, a friend, a relative, your social worker, someone from a voluntary organisation. They can give you moral support but also do useful things like taking notes, intervening if you get upset, helping if the person you care for needs attention. It is also useful to be able to compare impressions with someone else afterwards.

4. Consider where you would prefer the meeting to take place. Sometimes you feel more confident on your home ground. If it is important for the person you care for to be present, you will feel more comfortable attending to them at home. You may wish the person you are talking to to see the one you care for in their home setting. Sometimes the subject matter of the meeting is better suited to a more formal atmosphere. The important thing is that you should have some say in the matter.

5. Record the outcome of your discussion in some way. You may write a brief note and keep it with relevant correspondence; note the date of the discussion and who was present, for example 'Spoke to George Walters, Neighbourhood Officer, 21.10.92 re. bathroom adaptations for Joy. He said he would arrange a meeting at our flat with the occupational therapist. He will get in touch.' Then, if you have heard nothing in, say, two weeks, you know who promised what and whom to get back to.

6. It is often useful to write briefly to the person you spoke to, confirming what was agreed, eg:

24.6.9—

Ms A. Phillips,
Occupational Therapist,
Westshire Community Services Team,
3 Park Street,
Westbury

Copy to: Dr. Curtis, Liam's G.P.
Ms J. Devon, Liam's Social Worker.

Dear Ms Phillips,

Thank you for coming to see us today about the bathroom hoist for Liam.

I know you said funds were short, but it has taken four months since I first asked about the hoist just to get this appointment.

You saw how big Liam is. He will be ten soon and I can hardly lift him now. Unless we get this hoist soon, I am afraid my back will go again.

You said you would let me know within the month what the decision is. I want to let you know that if it is refused I shall appeal, as I cannot be expected to manage Liam at home unless I get this help.

Please let me know as soon as you have some news.

Yours sincerely,

MEETINGS

Sometimes groups of parents/carers meet with officials, councillors, and so forth, to discuss a problem, a cut in provision, or a request for a development of a service. When we were to be involved in such a meeting, we always met beforehand to plan our strategy. The officials, councillors, and others, will have had such a pre-meeting, so you need to be at least as well prepared. We would take our notes, correspondence, documents and so forth, along. If there were several officials present we would take one each and make notes of what they said; then we could compare notes afterwards and write a full account of the meeting. We often had the most complete account!

Sometimes it is possible to establish regular meetings with, say, the Chair of Social Services, or Education, to ensure that carers' views are taken seriously and fed into the planning process. These are more likely to happen if you have been able to build up a relationship with a particular councillor, by taking the person you care for to their surgery, writing to them for help, giving them information about disability. We found some councillors were able to take an informed interest once they had the information; they were not uncaring people but they simply did not know about some aspects of disability. Once they had grasped the issues as they affected actual people, they could be very supportive.

The other sort of meeting you may be involved in is one where you are meeting one or more professionals, perhaps to follow up a complaint you have made about an aspect of the service to the person you care for. It is very important to be clear who on 'their' side will be at the meeting. Then you need to make sure you are accompanied by at least one other person – a partner, friend, voluntary organisation member, advocate. Ask what the status of the meeting is; ask what the aims of the meeting are. If these differ from yours, read out your own notes. Those with you can take notes of what is said, leaving you free to concentrate on the discussion and getting your points over. These meetings need not be confrontational, but you also need to have the confidence to be assertive.

You have the right to ask for meetings, if you feel that that is the best way of sorting a matter out. During Kathy's first hospital admission after transfer to the adult hospital, everything that could possibly go wrong did. They could not get the diet right, they did not seem to know how to deal with fits, they could not seem to cope with the naso-gastric tube, they got arrangements muddled. Following her discharge we wrote outlining our concerns to Kathy's consultant. He met with us, and subsequently with ward staff to discuss our concerns and agree on how things would be managed in future.

It is sensible to try to sort out difficulties directly with the person concerned first, for example if you are dissatisfied with some aspect of care in a residential unit. If you do not get a positive response or if they say it happened because of reasons outside their control, then you need to go to the next step up. We used to draw diagrams for ourselves to understand the various levels of authority in residential establishments, Social Services department, and so on. If we did not get a satisfactory response on an issue, we would try the next most senior, filling in our diagram as we learned the various names and telephone extensions. An example:

PS: Principal Administrative Officer
Social Services Supplies
Extension 184.

JW:
who actually has authority to order certain items
Extension 486.

MN and **MS**:
Administrative Officers
(under JW)
Extension 487.

This was one section in the local authority. We were gradually able to build up our own diagram of the hierarchy of officers in Social Services. We could then see the chain of responsibility and work out whom it was most appropriate to call on a particular matter. It might sound like hard work, but it saved much time and frustration in the long run. As we learned the various names, it also made a faceless bureaucracy become more real, and individual officers were less likely to put us off or pass the buck, because they knew that we knew the set up.

Part Three

Tell Them About Me

CHAPTER 6

TELL THEM ABOUT ME – THE CARE BOOK

I found I had to tell many different people about Kathy, in all kinds of situations. She could not speak for herself, so she could not say how she felt at different times, how she liked to spend her time, what made her happy and comfortable. She could not explain where her pain and discomfort was. It was not always easy to tell from her cries and unhappy sounds whether she was really distressed, or bored and annoyed because things were not happening as she wished. She did not understand that some things she did, such as grabbing at interesting objects, pulling at strings or cloths, or pushing things aside could cause problems and even catastrophes.

She might have a new teacher, go for respite care, be admitted to hospital in an emergency. I carried a lot of information in my head and notes on bits of paper. I often wondered where to start, and how on earth to explain it all before they fell asleep. I began to make up a scrapbook with information about Kathy: what she was like when she was younger, what she looked like when she was well, what was distinctive about her personality, how she tried to communicate, what she enjoyed doing, as well as details about her daily care needs and medical requirements. I included photographs so that people would see her in a variety of moods, situations and states of health. This turned out to be a useful and convenient way of communicating a lot of information to a variety of people.

The care book, as I came to call it, needed to be updated from time to time, and it ran into several editions. Eventually, I found it more useful to use an A4 plastic-covered ring binder or booklet with transparent plastic sleeves. It was durable, would travel, and enabled individual items of information to be updated.

Professionals, especially doctors and nurses, often see someone when they are ill, upset, anxious, immobile, and it is vitally important for their expectations and decisions on management and treatment to know how that person can be in different circumstances.

It was also useful in some situations for the book to be used for reminders and reference, especially on the ward during a hospital admission and when new people began to work with Kathy: teachers, carers, physiotherapists and so on.

We took the care book out with us, not only to the situations described above, but also if we went out for the day or on holiday. Then, if we found ourselves in a worrying situation, likely to forget important details because we were concerned about Kathy's condition, the basic information was all to hand.

We tried to make sure that her care book really spoke for Kathy. In updating it we took account of changes, not just in her medical condition, but new skills and awareness. We involved her as much as possible when putting it together, and she liked to look at it.

This is how Kathy's care book was put together – the pages shown are mainly those explaining and illustrating Kathy and her care; some of the detailed sheets such as those on fits and diets appear in Chapter 8.

Contents

This makes it easy for carers to look up a topic quickly. It also gives an idea of the wide range of needs of the person you care for.

KATHY SIROCKIN : HER BOOK

The purpose of this book is:

1. To give you some basic information about Kathy

2. To give guidance on Kathy's basic care routines.

This explains what the book is for, and shows a photograph of Kathy on holiday, relaxed and well, to show carers how she could be at her best.

FAMILY , CARERS, FRIENDS

PARENTS

Pat and Battie Fitton,
2 Heyworth Road,
Clapton,
London E5 8 DR.
081 - 986 - 6587

WORK: 081-801- 0091
(Pat)

Kathy stays with us
most weekends and
school holidays

INDEPENDENT LIVING SCHEME

95 Kendal House,
Priory Green,
London NI 4 DF.
071 - 837 - 2048

KATHY'S GUARDIANS
(in the event of parents' death)

Jean and Norman Willson,
33 Cornelia Street,
London N7.
071 - 607- 8327

G.P.

DR J. JONES
21 EXLEY STREET,
LONDON NI.
071 - 111 - 2345
APPTS: 071-676-8910

HOSPITAL

GREENBANK HOSPITAL,
Woodley Drive,
London ...
081 — 767 - 7890

CONSULTANTS

Dr A. B. Curtis
(Gastro- enterology)

Dr D. F. Gilligan
(Rheumatology)

Dr H. I. Jackman
(Neurology)

This gives the essential contact details for Kathy's family, and close friends who would supervise her care if we both died. The names of the GP, hospital and consultants have been changed. This information meant that wherever Kathy was, in an emergency carers could contact those close to her and those who could give medical advice. Often a talk over the telephone would be enough to sort the situation out. If not, we would want to join her as quickly as possible in hospital or wherever she might be.

Kathy's Condition

Kathy was born on 17. 11. 63. She had cerebral palsy and severe mental retardation from birth. Cause unknown.

(← Aged three)

At age four and a half she developed severe rheumatoid arthritis. All limbs were severely affected. Kathy never walked again.

(↓ Aged four)

At age nine Kathy had an operation on her left hip to remedy dislocation and infection. Result: left hip fixed, sitting more difficult, standing and walking impossible.

At age ten Kathy began to have convulsions. She now has many different types of fit.

At age sixteen (←—) Kathy developed severe inflammatory bowel disease, subsequently diagnosed as Crohn's disease. RE-DIAGNOSED AUGUST 1990 AS COLLAGENOUS COLITIS, FOLLOWING COLONOSCOPY AND BIOPSIES. Kathy has had a naso-gastric tube permanently since 1984. (age 20)

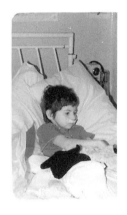

This explains very briefly Kathy's various disabilities and medical conditions. It gives the information in date order, so that readers can see how life got more difficult for her as time went on.

KATHY'S   MEDICATION   30. 7. 91

EPILIM :	to control fits (anti-convulsant)
TEGRETOL :	as above
CLOBAZAM :	to control floppy fits
PREDNISOLONE :	to relieve inflammation and pain in the joints and the bowel (steroid)
NAPROSYN :	to relieve inflammation and pain in the joints
PARACETEMOL :	to relieve pain
KETOVITE LIQUID :	fat soluble vitamin supplement
KETOVITE TABLETS	water soluble vitamin supplement

RE - ORDERING

Pat and Barrie re-order supplies (+ creams, Dioralyte, soya, Fortisan, plasters etc) monthly from GP; they take the prescription to their pharmacist and take supplies as necessary to Kendal House.

IF YOU RUN SHORT OF ANY ITEM

Phone Pat and Barrie first to see if they have it.
If not, phone surgery (Dr Jones 071-111-2345) but you may have to allow 48 hours notice.

DO CHECK

Each time you give medication, that there are adequate supplies.
Try not to leave it until the last minute to let us or the GP know you need further supplies.

GIVING MEDICATION

Kathy's current medication is in a box on the top shelf of the wall cupboard nearest the window. Spares are at the back of that shelf.
A current dosage list is kept in the same place.
A record diary for giving medication is kept in the same place.
Please sign for the time and date you give medication.

TEMPORARY CHANGES

EG antibiotic; suspending use of a drug; temporary change in dosage — record on POST-IT on medication dosage sheet.

NB PARACETEMOL

a   Record all doses given
b. Check any other item newly prescribed or given for paracetemol content eg cough medicine.
Check with G.P. if in doubt to avoid over-dosing.

This explains the purpose of Kathy's various medicines. It gives details of how to re-order supplies. It explains how to record when you give her medication, and what to do when she may be on a drug temporarily, such as an antibiotic, or when a drug is stopped for a trial period. Full details of medication, arrangements for giving it and dosages are in Chapter 8.

What sort of person is Kathy?

Kathy has a powerful personality, and a strong sense of her own identity and worth.

She is responsive to physical contact, talk and play.

Mood changes are frequent and can be extreme.

Bad moods are due to one of the following :-

1. Pain

2. Discomfort

3. Hunger — Kathy has a swift throughput!

4. Epileptic activity — this can make Kathy morose, or can cause extreme distress with screaming.

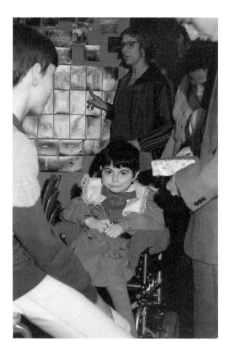

The idea of this page is to establish Kathy as a real individual, not a collection of problems. This page shows pictures of Kathy, one very happy and relaxed, the other very grumpy. A description of her personality is given and an explanation of how and why her moods may change rapidly.

Kathy   likes

* Playing with toys, especially on the floor

* Listening to music (baroque, early, classical, rather than pop)

* cuddles

* sitting sociably with a group — at home, visiting friends, in the pub, in a restaurant.

The next two pages explain and show the various things Kathy enjoys doing. The photographs help others to see what a wide range of interests she has and how she enjoys being out and about.

Kathy   also   likes

* Going for walks
* Travelling in vehicles

* Going on holiday (especially in France)

* Swimming (that is, splashing and floating with armbands on)

Communication

Kathy will make eye contact and can be very sociable.

She is more secure and sociable in familiar surroundings. She may "shut off" in a new or worrying situation.

She picks up "social clues" — laughter, excitement, anger, preparations, etc.

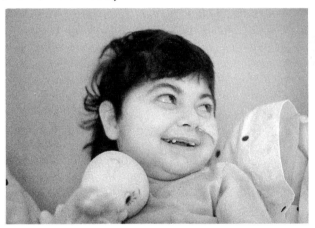

KATHY HAS NO SPEECH. She communicates her needs in very basic ways:-

1. crying — disapproval, need.
2. smiling and laughing, clapping hands — approval, pleasure.
3. pointing, leaning, pushing, pulling — to indicate a need, or reject something offered, eg a drink; to change a situation eg. to get you to change a music tape.

She also has a range of happy and sad sounds.

This page explains that Kathy does not talk and describes how she communicates her needs and wishes. It also explains why she does not always seem to want to communicate, and how she works out what is going on around her.

IN HOSPITAL

BASIC NEEDS

If Kathy is admitted to hospital, nursing staff need to be made aware of the basic initial needs for hygiene and safety.

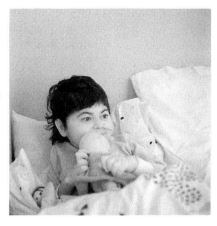

1. Pads, plastic bed sheets and draw sheets, as she is DOUBLY INCONTINENT.

2. Cot sides, as she has little SENSE OF DANGER.

3. Ripple mattress as she develops pressure sores easily.

4. Special diet — milk and lactose free, low fat, low fibre.

   SEE DIET SHEETS ON FOLLOWING PAGES.

WARNING: Keep equipment — cotton wool, instruments, medication, etc. WELL OUT OF KATHY's REACH.
She will grab anything interesting.

This page summarises the immediate things to see to if Kathy was admitted to hospital. It was mainly for occasions when she might be admitted and we were not there. It reminds carers and hospital staff that certain things need to be seen to straight away because of Kathy's special needs.

Kathy Feeds herself

She uses a spoon
or fingers, as
appropriate.
She can pick up a
cup to give herself
a drink.

These pages show pictures of Kathy eating with a spoon and with her fingers. There is an explanation of how she gives herself food and drink, what she enjoys and what she dislikes. There are some suggestions for when she is having problems with eating. There is a reminder that her naso-gastric tube is not her usual method of getting nourishment and that normal eating and drinking should be tried first.

FEEDING:

Kathy feeds herself with a small spoon from a bowl once her food is chopped
into small pieces.
She must be in a good sitting position in her special wheelchair with food
easily reached. You may need to put a tray between her chair and the table top.
Kathy also finger feeds bread, cold meats, fruit, etc. She likes to eat a
large boiled potato from her hand sometimes.
Kathy drinks from an ordinary cup or glass. As well as Formula-S she drinks
Blackcurrant, rose hip, fruit juice, squash. She can lift and hold a cup to
drink but sometimes drops it when she has finished. Recently she has preferred
to have a cup lifted to her mouth.

LIKES and DISLIKES

Kathy likes boiled eggs best.
Next best is smoked salmon.
Then plain meals with meat or fish and potatoes and cauliflower.
It is not worth making her special cakes and biscuits as she rarely eats them.
If Kathy is not eating it is always worth trying her with freshly made toast
and Tomor.

PROBLEMS WITH EATING

Kathy gets nausea sometimes and also discomfort and pain. Sometimes this means
she won't eat at all. However it is worth trying two things:
  (a) use a tissue to empty her mouth of accumulated dribble or mucus
  (b) use a tissue to clear away any accumulated food from the roof of her
       mouth.

Sometimes she wants a drink; have it close so she can indicate.
Sometimes she wants someone else's food. Say "No" firmly and if necessary push
her back from the table for a while before trying again.
Kathy is very responsive to social clues about eating. She eats regularly with
us in restaurants and usually behaves in an acceptable manner.

N.B.
THE NASO-GASTRIC TUBE IS MAINLY FOR DRUGS AND FOR FLUIDS WHEN KATHY WON'T DRINK

We always offer a drink orally before putting it down the tube. We aim for
Kathy to take at least a litre of fluid in 24 hours- not all soya, sometimes
blackcurrant, rosehip, fruit juice, squash. e.g.
    7 a.m. Breakfast always Formula-S
    mid-morning; juice etc. as above
    lunch; juice etc. with meal; soya if food refused.
    mid afternoon: juice etc. as above
    supper: juice etc. with meal; soya if food refused
    10 p.m. : always 200 ml Formula-S with last drugs.

F I T S

Kathy now has a complex pattern of fit activity.

The two main groups are :-

1. CONVULSIONS

Typical whole body seizures involving all four limbs, going blue, difficulty regaining breath. Rectal valium given in 5 mg units.

Detailed notes on following pages.

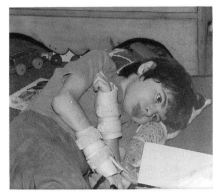

2. Floppy episodes, long spasms, sudden deep "sleeps", extreme distress with screaming and throwing herself about. The floppy episodes are potentially dangerous.

Detailed notes on following pages.

Kathy also has absences.

Combinations of different types of fit are increasingly common.

This gives a summary of the main types of fit Kathy has, for quick reference. It shows two pictures of Kathy recovering from fits. It refers carers to more detailed notes when they have time or need more information. These are in Chapter 8.

Kathy's   Naso - Gastric   Tube

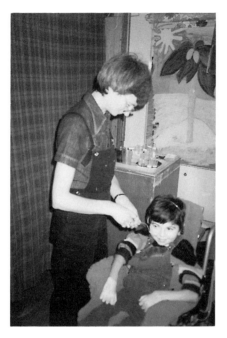

Since June 1984 Kathy has had a naso-gastric tube permanently:-

a. For administration of all drugs.

b. Administration of fluids when she won't drink.

c. Feeding eg. soya, flexical, when she is unwell and won't eat.

The NGT is <u>not</u> her main method of feeding, unless she is very ill.

The big advantage of the NGT is that Kathy does not get dehydrated on days when the bowel is causing problems. It also allows feeding in periods when she is feeling too unwell to eat, avoiding too much weight loss. The need for hospital admission is therefore much reduced.

This page explains why Kathy now has a naso-gastric tube, and how it has helped her.

USING THE N.G.T.

You can give drugs and fluids when Kathy is in her special wheelchair, or in bed.

She needs to be secure and comfortable, and to have something to occupy her.

Generally we find the procedure easier to manage when she is in her chair.

However, we always give late - night drugs in bed, to avoid moving her after.

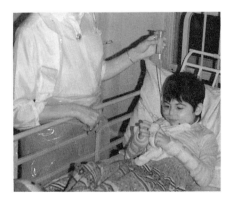

These pages give step by step instructions for where to give tube feeds, how to prepare medication, how to give feeds and what to do if there are problems.

Getting Ready

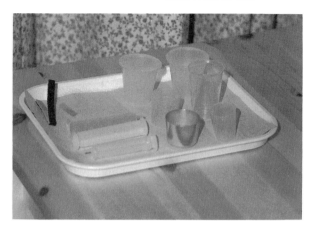

(1) We measure syrups out separately.
   Dissolve aspirins and prednisolone in water.
   Crush other tablets and mix with soluble ones.

(2)
Have
ready:
plain
water,
litmus,
20 ml
syringe.

(3)

Aspirate
small
amount
of fluid
and test
if it
turns
litmus
pink.

(4)
Syringe syrups down SLOWLY.
Let soluble tablets and fluids go down by GRAVITY.
Finally let 5 ml plain water through syringe.

Problems with the NGT

1. The tube does cause a build-up of mucus due to irritation. This makes Kathy vomit sometimes, which clears the problem for a while.

2. Kathy sometimes pulls it out — if it is irritating her, or sometimes to get attention.

IT MUST, OF COURSE, BE REPLACED EACH WEEK.

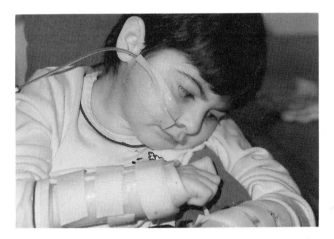

It helps to replace the plaster when it comes loose.
We use waterproof plaster.
Cut a piece to fit snugly up to her nostril, trying not to leave a loop.

Kathy knows what the tube is for. She will indicate at times when she needs her aspirin, and is often pleased to have fluid down the tube when she is not drinking.

IMPORTANT

Leave Kathy in the same position after tube-feeding as long as possible. In the day time she sometimes "flops out" in her chair after tube feeding. We leave her in the chair UNLESS she doesn't wake after about 30 minutes or her breathing seems very laboured — in these cases put her in the recovery position and observe.

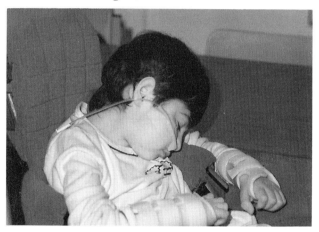

At night we prepare her completely before the last drugs — wash, clean teeth, nappy changed, in bed — leaving her without physical disturbance after the last NGT administration.

It is at this time that she has been prone to serious fitting following NGT administration — floppy, blue, vomiting episodes, resulting sometimes in her becoming very cold, pulse slowing, blood pressure dropping, breathing shallow, etc.

Nappy Area

Kathy's skin is thin and she has old bedsore scars.

She has systemic thrush which is kept in check by changing the treatment creams at intervals.

Her persistent diarrhoea makes soreness more likely.

AT EACH NAPPY CHANGE

Use only tissue and damp cotton wool. Dry thoroughly with cotton wool.

Soap should not be used more than once a day.

VASOGEN CREAM applied to nappy area after each change.

METANIUM OINTMENT instead if Kathy is very sore.

CANESTEN CREAM ⎫ applied to vulva and vaginal area 3
ALTERNATED WITH ⎬ times a day, for the thrush.
NYSTAN ⎭

With regular changing and this regime Kathy's skin stays in reasonable condition. It can break down very quickly and is then very hard to heal.

This page explains the problems arising from Kathy's double incontinence, and how they are made worse by her medical condition and some of her medication. It gives basic instructions for changing her pads, cleaning and creaming. It emphasises that usually there is no need for Kathy to get sore if this routine is followed at every change.

SKIN CARE

Kathy's skin is thin and delicate after prolonged steroid treatment.

She also has vitiligo, with extensive de-pigmented areas.

SOAP : Glycerine best, or mild baby or simple soap.

NO BUBBLE BATH or bath additives, except salt.

MOISTURE LOTION all over body after bath.

MOUTH AREA creamed at intervals during the day, as it breaks down very easily.

SUN SCREENS   Kathy has de-pigmented areas on her face, hands, feet and body.

IF she is exposed to the sun even in winter, she must have sun screens applied:

SPECTRABAN applied with cotton wool before dressing

UVISTAT On top, and at intervals during day.

IF not, she will burn on the de-pigmented areas.

Kathy loves her bath. She gets valuable exercise while splashing and playing.
It is easier to wash her hair in the bath.

This page explains why Kathy's skin is delicate and gives clear guidance on washing and bathing, and on the use of moisture lotion and sun screen. It also emphasises how much Kathy enjoys her bath, and how it gives her exercise as well as fun.

Pressure   Sores

These can start at any time, especially when Kathy is unwell or recovering from fits, when she may be in one position for a long time.

Look for a round, reddened area, slightly raised or depressed according to site. This is most likely to be on the buttocks. Skin feels soft, almost sticky.

(1) Dab surgical spirit on gently, on and around the sore.

(2) Cover with a fresh Melolin dressing, shiny side to skin. Do not fix with plaster if it can be kept in place by the nappy — the surrounding area is delicate too and can be damaged by plaster coming on and off.

(3) Encourage Kathy to position herself off the sore area.

(4) Expose to air if at all feasible ie if Kathy is asleep for some hours — we have done this in the garden when it has been sunny!

(5) Observe progress and seek medical help if the sore does not improve within 2 or 3 days, or gets worse.

This page explains what to look for if Kathy is beginning to develop pressure sores. It gives detailed instructions on how to treat any that are starting and what to do if there is no improvement.

Bruising

Kathy bruises very easily now.

This is thought to be due to fragile blood vessel walls.

Platelets should be checked regularly, and if especially extensive bruising occurs.

Do not restrict Kathy's activities because of this problem. Independent movement is essential to her, as it helps to minimise osteoporosis as well as preventing worse stiffness.

Note any particularly deep or extensive bruises. Use ARNICA ointment on the worst bruises – it soothes and helps to clear them up more quickly.

Kathy's eyes are often very bloodshot, and sometimes she will develop a small haemotoma in one eye. This is thought to be part of the same problem. If there is a haemotoma get the eyes checked by a doctor, in case there is a serious problem.

This explains why Kathy bruises so easily. The main purpose of this page is to reassure carers that she should be allowed to move as much as she can, even at the risk of some bruises. She enjoys movement and it helps to prevent other medical problems. Details are given of how to treat any bruises. There is also a note on what to do if there seems to be bruising in her eye.

PHYSIOTHERAPY

Kathy must have physiotherapy twice daily, especially when she is in hospital.

If not, she will rapidly stiffen up, and it will be very difficult to make her comfortable.

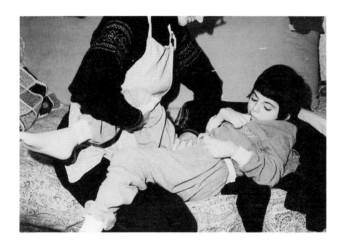

Kathy can get a lot of exercise through play. However, it is important that the movements are checked regularly through her formal exercise programme; details on the following pages. Mobility of her right hip is especially important to preserve her ability to sit.

Sometimes Kathy needs postural drainage if she has a lot of mucus or is "chesty".

This page emphasises how vital it is for Kathy to have physiotherapy. It also points out that even though normal movement is important, the exercises need to be done as a routine. There is also a note about special physiotherapy if she is chesty, and a note of the telephone number of the community physiotherapist.

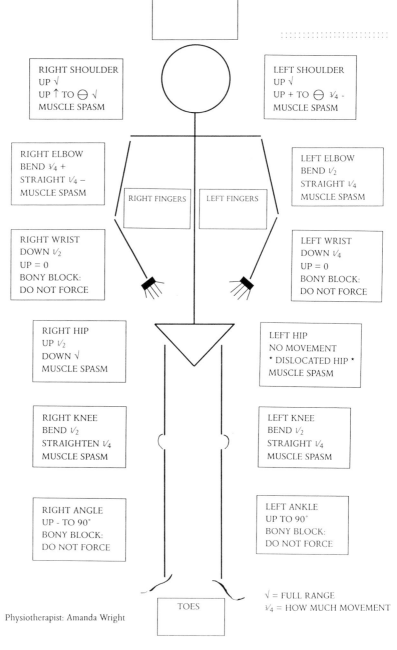

RIGHT SHOULDER
UP √
UP ↑ TO ⊖ √
MUSCLE SPASM

LEFT SHOULDER
UP √
UP + TO ⊖ ¾ -
MUSCLE SPASM

RIGHT ELBOW
BEND ¾ +
STRAIGHT ¼ –
MUSCLE SPASM

LEFT ELBOW
BEND ½
STRAIGHT ¼
MUSCLE SPASM

RIGHT FINGERS

LEFT FINGERS

RIGHT WRIST
DOWN ½
UP = 0
BONY BLOCK:
DO NOT FORCE

LEFT WRIST
DOWN ¼
UP = 0
BONY BLOCK:
DO NOT FORCE

RIGHT HIP
UP ½
DOWN √
MUSCLE SPASM

LEFT HIP
NO MOVEMENT
* DISLOCATED HIP *
MUSCLE SPASM

RIGHT KNEE
BEND ½
STRAIGHTEN ¼
MUSCLE SPASM

LEFT KNEE
BEND ½
STRAIGHT ¼
MUSCLE SPASM

RIGHT ANGLE
UP - TO 90°
BONY BLOCK:
DO NOT FORCE

LEFT ANKLE
UP TO 90°
BONY BLOCK:
DO NOT FORCE

TOES

√ = FULL RANGE
¼ = HOW MUCH MOVEMENT

Physiotherapist: Amanda Wright

This shows very clearly for each part of the body how much movement to expect when you are doing Kathy's exercises, or carrying out other activities for her. It is especially useful for carers doing the exercises for the first time, so they avoid forcing tender joints.

MENSTRUATION

We think Kathy menstruates.

After her illness in 1984 she put on weight and her breasts developed. She then began to have slight bleeding at irregular intervals. It seems likely that the weight gain triggered the hormonal change.

She does not bleed much, and as she is in nappies no extra precautions are needed, except to be even more careful about hygiene when changing.

It is difficult to say whether her mood changes with the cycle — her mood changes seem much more likely to be due to epileptic activity. In addition, the cycle is not regular.

Kathy's GP thinks the bleeding may be part of the same process that is causing the bruising and bleeding in the eyes.

Ring the date in the diary and make a note if you discover any bleeding.

This page discusses the uncertain nature of Kathy's periods, gives a simple method of recording any bleeding, and explains how to deal with it.

SPLINTS

Kathy's wrists are dropping due to the arthritis.

The joints will eventually fuse.
It is important that they fuse in a useful position, not folded over.

DAY SPLINTS must be worn during waking hours, except for meal times.

Kathy now has different ones from those shown in the picture — light brown elastic, with a stiffening metal insert.

The principle is the same.

Kathy tolerates them well.

NIGHT SPLINTS are paddles made of hard plastic, fastened with straps. Put these on just before you leave her at night. She tries to take them off — and often succeeds!

This explains how important Kathy's wrist splints are and describes the difference between the day and night splints.

WHEELCHAIR

Kathy has a matrix moulded to her shape, fitted on a NHS push chair base with 4 x 12" wheels.   Ref. no. LH 31880.

The matrix is adjustable to further changes in her position. Any adjustments are carried out at the Hackney Wheelchair Clinic, Hackney Hospital, Homerton High Street, E9 6BE. Tel: 081-533-6896.

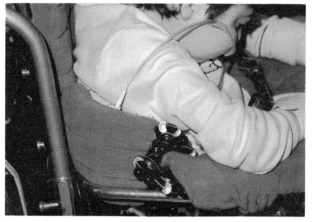

Kathy uses her chair at mealtimes, for walks, journeys, and for sitting sociably in company. The rest of the time she prefers to be on the floor.
Tyres need pumping up from time to time; bicycle pump on floor of wardrobe in Kendal House.
Take a puncture kit when you go out.
The matrix and base need washing down regularly.
The matrix cover needs changing frequently — DON'T tumble dry it! ☒ Machine wash delicate, hang to dry.

CHECK BRAKES WEEKLY: if not secure, call repairer.
(Details in diary)

This gives a brief summary of what Kathy's wheelchair is like, with the reference number, and details of where to get adjustments and repairs. This is important because any old wheelchair will not do. There is a note about when to use the wheelchair, and brief details on how to keep it clean and in good repair.

CHAPTER 7

DIARIES

Diaries are increasingly used between carers and schools, between families and other carers, and in any situation where several people or agencies are dealing with the person with the disability. They are essential for anyone with complex conditions. We liked to record how Kathy was at the beginning of the day, and for others caring for her to record any changes, for example if she cheered up after starting off unhappy or distressed. Sometimes we needed to tell a doctor when vomiting started, how many episodes there had been, if bowel or appetite patterns had changed, or how many fits she had during the day and what type they were. It was also important for us to know whether Kathy had received her medication at the usual time, and how much food and fluids she had taken during the whole day. We sometimes needed to track back over a longer period to see if any problem such as the fits was getting worse or changing its nature over a period of time. You may need to draw together such information from your own observations and those of others such as other carers, teachers, bus escorts.

One page a day diaries are compact but there is not always enough room for all the required information, and they tend to fall apart as the year goes on. An example of a page is given below:

1991   *February*

Monday 25

Kathy was asleep when I arrived; stirred while being given Amoxil then woke up a little surprised to see me. Changed, b/m medium sticky. Kathy ate all her breakfast – 1 egg, slice of bread, no drink. 150 ml soya ngt plus drugs. Kathy was quiet in the bath, some fit activity. Dried and creamed, dressed. 150 ml soya ngt. We took Kathy out into the park and sat in the sunshine. Kathy was sleepy, also some fit activity. Kathy was checked, dry. Kathy was slightly sick on her bed and refused her meal of ham and crispbread. Aspirin plus 100 ml camomile tea ngt. I let Kathy lay down as she was grumpy; remained quiet while lying down. Changed b/m small loose. Stayed in bed but not asleep. Changed ngt plaster.

5 pm woke up after sleepy afternoon. b/m very sticky; changed.

Kathy ate a large meal this evening of liver, mashed potato, mixed veg and gravy. Drugs ngt plus 150 ml water. V.slightly wet at 8 p.m. and changed. Kathy spent time after dinner watching Dan wash up in the kitchen. She fell asleep on the floor in the lounge so put to bed. She stayed awake later listening to music. Large b/m 10.20 p.m. Drugs given at 11 pm plus 220 ml water.

We used an agreed system of abbreviations – ngt meant fluids were given through Kathy's tube, usually because she would not drink; b/m was bowel movement. We kept a tally of amounts of fluid given to Kathy in a column ruled down the side of each page. She could get dehydrated very easily, especially on hot days, and it was important to be able to see at the end of a day how much fluid in total she had taken. It was important to record amounts, size and nature of bowel movements as any increase may mean Kathy's bowel disease was more active. 'Fit activity' meant generalised activity such as flickering eyes, twitching, absences; carers recorded more precisely if Kathy had convulsions or long floppy periods, as follows:

Kathy was difficult to wake and while being changed went into a drop fit app.10.55. No response to movement, eyes dilated, cheeks cold. Movement app.11.30, opened her eyes at 11.55 and then went into a normal sleep.

A loose leaf folder with pre-printed sheets may be more useful than a bound diary. It also allows information to be itemised and retrieved more easily:

You can make up your own headings according to the needs of the person you care for. If you have your own typewriter or word processor or know someone who has, you can design it exactly as you want. You will then need to have the required number of sheets photocopied or printed. It works out more expensive than using a ready-made diary but is probably easier to use and read.

It is useful to include a sheet with basic contact names and telephone numbers in both the care book and the diary. This information may be kept by others caring for the person in their files, but it is useful to have it in a compact and readily accessible form.

| |

Hair Wash	Nails	B/O	Outings	Activities	Exercises	Medication
						a.m.
						p.m.
						p.m.

Shopping Needed

Lists will vary with the requirements of the person, but an example is as follows:

NAME(S)

Kathy Sirockin	Address
	Home telephone number
Parents/Next of Kin	Address
	Home Number
	Work Number(s)
Emergency contact	Address
	Telephone Number
Guardians in case of Parents' Death	Address
	Telephone Number
GP	. . . .
Consultant	. . . .
Emergency arrangements	. . . .
eg. special hospital number,	. . . .
named doctor, etc.	. . . .
Community Physiotherapist	. . . .
Social Worker	. . . .

The diary is only of use if everyone concerned reads it and makes appropriate entries. When Kathy came home from school, centre, residential unit, and so forth, I read the entries since she had been away, to catch up with how she had been and what had been going on. I expected her other carers, teachers or whoever to do the same. Otherwise, they might not be aware that she had had a difficult night and was very tired, or that there were special circumstances to watch out for that day. Sometimes Kathy had started antibiotics, and whoever was taking over her care would need to know this. It made me angry if other carers said they had only just come on duty after a few days leave and had not realised what the current situation was – that was exactly what the diary was for! Similarly, everyone making entries needs to make them in clear language and as soon after the event they are describing as possible. This is particularly important when describing epileptic episodes.

We also appreciated it when carers wrote about something really positive, or some development they had noticed, which illustrated just how much trouble they were taking to communicate with Kathy. Some comments gave a flavour of the day, and also illustrated a warm relationship:

> *I am still trying to feed Kathy but she doesn't want any food. When I went to the phone Kathy dropped her dinner tray and thought that really amusing. 3 p.m. Kathy hasn't had lunch but hasn't stopped laughing since the tray accident.*

It is also important to note appointments in the diary – hospital, physiotherapists, social events. All those involved in aspects of care of the person with disabilities should get used to checking these well before the date, to avoid double booking and to make sure that special arrangements, for example transport, are made.

Used carefully, the diary can be a link between various carers and establishments. It can help to make care more consistent for someone who may be attended to by several different people during one day. It can also ensure a more consistent approach to developing skills and identifying interests and strengths. It can be very helpful for carers in one setting to see how the person with disabilities responds in other situations. If the diary is taken to appointments, it can be used to check that up-to-date and accurate information is given about the person you care for.

CHAPTER 8

INFORMATION SHEETS

Carers forget how much they learn about keeping someone with complex needs happy, comfortable, well and safe. They learn, develop and invent all kinds of systems, strategies and arrangements to make this possible. We went through this process, and we learned from the ideas that Kathy's other carers had. We began to write this information down, keeping copies in her care book and giving copies to others who looked after her. These information sheets were reminders if any of us forgot some things; they enabled useful information to be recorded permanently; and they were especially useful for people new to Kathy. There were two main types, those for constant needs, such as dealing with Kathy's epilepsy, and those produced for particular situations, for example when she might have an acute illness.

CONSTANT NEEDS

Epilepsy

If you are caring for someone with complex epilepsy, an information sheet explaining the various types of fit and methods of dealing with them is important. Information and guidelines are available from various sources; there are details at the end of the chapter. We drew Kathy's up after close observation of her reactions during different types of fit, and discussions with her doctors about appropriate methods of dealing with them. Carers can be very frightened by seeing fits, especially if it is a first time for them, or if they do not know the person very well. Clear explanations of what is happening and guidance as to appropriate action is essential to avoid panic and possible threat to life. This is particularly important when someone has different types of fit, not always requiring the same response. Kathy's epilepsy became more complex as she got older, and then the straightforward guidance on how to deal with a grand mal convulsion was not always appropriate. Some extracts from the information sheet about Kathy's fits are given below:

DESCRIPTION

Grand mal convulsions:

Face changes colour to pale or grey; limbs go rigid and then jerk convulsively, eyes may be staring or half-closed, teeth clenched, often moaning sounds. Often goes blue. May take time to get her breath back, gasping and sighing sounds. Usually but not always followed by 20 minutes or so loss of consciousness, then deep sleep.

N.B. When recording duration of fit, note only time of actual fit (rarely more than two minutes) don't include comatose period after.

ACTION

Lay Kathy on her side in the recovery position at once, to ease breathing and avoid inhalation of dribble or vomit.

Give 5 mg rectal valium as soon as possible, even during fit. Repeat if further convulsions follow, up to a total of 20 mg.

CALL AN AMBULANCE IF:

Fits don't stop after 20 mg valium

Kathy is still blue

Kathy has breathing difficulties (try pulling her lower jaw forward with thumb and forefinger to loosen tongue from roof of mouth).

Leave Kathy to sleep – avoid waking or moving her for as long as possible.

N.B. If Kathy has more than one episode of convulsions within 24 hours she should be checked by a doctor in case she has an infection.

During the next few years we noticed that Kathy had other types of fit as well – absences, shaking, dribbling/choking episodes, spasms, brief jerks of the limbs and flickering eyes. During a period of illness when she was 21 she began to have a very alarming type of fit, which we and her carers eventually referred to as 'drop fits'. Although these were not dramatic in the same way as the convulsions, the consequences seemed to be even more alarming. After rushing her to hospital twice when she seemed to be in deep shock, we collected our observations and worked out the best way to manage these episodes. The notes below proved very useful:

TYPE-TWO FITS (DROP FITS)

Start with a facial twitch and change of colour to pale or grey, then suddenly goes very floppy. Can be deeply unconscious usually for 20–30 minutes, but sometimes for several hours. These fits are most likely to follow administration of drugs and fluids by NGT, changing of nappy, baths, changes of position such as getting in and out of a vehicle.

On some occasions these fits have had alarming consequences – Kathy's temperature has fallen rapidly, pulse slowed down, breathing shallow, blood pressure falls, copious vomiting. In recent months they have been less dramatic.

ACTION

As soon as you notice onset, or if you find Kathy floppy, lay her on her side in the recovery position and observe carefully until she comes round. Sometimes she wakes, sometimes she eventually goes into a proper sleep.

KEEP HER WARM AND STILL.

If you notice she continues to be very cold or pulse is slow, breathing shallow, continued vomiting, etc. CALL AN AMBULANCE.

NO VALIUM TO BE GIVEN – this may depress breathing further.

If you are caring for someone with epilepsy, you may notice over time that certain circumstances make some fits more or less likely. It is worth making notes about this so that everyone who may care for her is aware of those circumstances.

It cannot be emphasised too strongly that all who care for someone with epilepsy must agree to a consistent system of recording fit activity. If a diary is in use, this is probably the best place, although a fit chart can be useful, especially if there seem to be changes in the usual pattern. You can draw up a fit chart to suit the circumstances and condition of the person you care for – this is just an example:

Date	Time	Brief description of fit including length	Action Taken	Result
. . . . . .	. . . . .	. . . .	. . . .	. . . .
. . . . . .	. . . . .	. . . .	. . . .	. . . .

Special Diets

When Kathy first became ill with bowel disease, we found that certain foods made her worse. During the next few years while the doctors worked to get an accurate diagnosis and gave her treatment, we gradually built up a picture of the kind of diet that seemed to keep her more comfortable and kept the diarrhoea under some control.

Carers needed to understand the principles of the diet, and then to see how it worked in practice, when giving drinks and meals. They also needed to have notes as a reminder when they were checking whether a particular item was suitable, or when advising a cook in a communal kitchen in a residential establishment. The principles were outlined first:

KATHERINE SIROCKIN: DIET SHEET

Lactose and milk free; low residue; lowish fat.

Milk and all manufactured products containing milk, casein, whey, butter etc. must be excluded from the diet.

AIMS OF THE DIET:

1. To exclude food thought to cause inflammatory reactions, eg. lactose, milk, milk products and all milk-containing manufactured foods.

2. To exclude food thought to exacerbate inflammation eg. excess fat.

3. To exclude food thought to make it more painful and difficult to pass food through a narrowed gut eg. high fibre.

4. The diet should be as high in calories as possible.

We then used information given by the hospital to list Foods Allowed and Foods Forbidden in two columns. We drew up a list of sample menus to encourage everyone to give Kathy as much variety as possible:

SAMPLE DAILY DIETS

BREAKFAST:

Usually a boiled egg plus one or two slices bread or toast with Tomor. Kathy does not like jam or honey on bread or toast. Sometimes permitted cereals with sugar and Formula-S. Kathy usually drinks 200 to 400 ml Formula-S at breakfast.

LUNCH/SUPPER

Boiled/baked potatoes, minced beef, cauliflower, permitted gravy.

Boiled/baked potatoes, casseroled beef/chicken/liver, cauliflower.

Boiled/baked potatoes, boiled or grilled white fish, cauliflower.

Grilled chicken breast, boiled/baked potatoes, cauliflower.

Boiled white rice with permitted meat and vegetable pieces.

Soft boiled egg chopped into mashed potato and cauliflower.

SOUPS:

Liquidise liver, potato, tinned asparagus, cauliflower, etc. singly or in combination. Kathy will eat with toast fingers.

UNCOOKED:

Bread/crispbread with cold lean meat, smoked salmon, tinned salmon or tuna, pipped and skinned pieces of cucumber and tomato.

AFTERS:

Kathy does not much like puddings, cakes and biscuits. Occasionally she will eat baked rice, ground rice, custard, all made with Formula-S; home made sorbet.

She enjoys pipped and peeled grapes, fresh or tinned lychees, melon, peeled apple, orange segments without pith.

We found that once carers understood the need for the diet and the basic principles, they were often very creative in providing a varied diet. They sought out dairy-free ice creams, sorbets and yogurt, found soya-based carob confectionary instead of chocolate, and took a lot of trouble to prepare salads and fruit. Kathy did not find it easy to adapt to her restricted diet at first. She loved cheese and ice cream, and although she came to accept substitutes she still wanted them when she saw them. Once on holiday in France we walked into a town square which was one entire cheese market – Kathy shouted with delight, but wailed in protest when we hurriedly retreated.

As with other things, Kathy's increasing maturity made her more ready to cope with such restrictions eventually. There were more problems with the diet in hospital than elsewhere. I have referred to this issue in more detail in Chapter 20.

Physiotherapy

We found the community physiotherapy approach more helpful with Kathy. She needed daily exercise routines to check her movements in her limbs, head and neck. But it was also useful to talk with physiotherapists and carers about how we could help her to exercise in daily activities such as baths, swimming, playing on the floor, encouraging her to reach during meals or when she went out. We all felt we needed notes to remind us of the basic exercises. The clearest to follow was the diagram giving parts of the body and describing the exercise for each. (This is in the 'Care Book' chapter – a simple but effective information sheet).

SPECIAL SITUATIONS

Kathy might have a particular episode such as, loss of appetite, or vomiting, not requiring hospitalisation but needing special attention. It was useful to draw up a separate sheet giving specific details of care required, what changes to look out for and report, when to contact the GP and so on. It could also be useful where new medication was introduced to explain what side effects to look for, what to record, and so on. Here is an example of a sheet drawn up to advise on preventing Kathy from becoming dehydrated in warm weather when she was unwell.

- 8 JUL 1991　　　6. 7. 91

KATHY'S FLUID INTAKE

KATHY NEEDS REGULAR FLUIDS TO REPLACE THOSE LOST THROUGH HER BOWEL DISEASE.

UNLESS SHE GETS:-

* ADEQUATE AMOUNTS
* AT FREQUENT INTERVALS
* OF THE RIGHT SORT

SHE WILL QUICKLY BECOME DEHYDRATED:-

DRAWN LOOK
LISTLESS
SKIN PINCHED (SHOWS FOLDS)
BLACK UNDER EYES
MISERABLE

SHE SHOULD ALWAYS HAVE COW AND GOAT SOYA FOR BREAKFAST. GIVE FORTISON IF SHE MISSES A MEAL...

[drawing] = 200 ml / person

GIVE 1½ 100 ML AT A TIME - 50 ML MORE FREQUENTLY IF SHE IS RETCHING.

OK AT OTHER TIMES JUICE, CAMOMILE TEA, ETC.

BUT [MOST IMPORTANT]

ON A HOT DAY GIVE NOT [DIORALYTE] WHEN GIVING SOYA OR FORTISON

JUICE OR WATER WILL WASH OUT ELECTROLYTES (ESSENTIAL CHEMICALS) THE CELL WILL NOT RETAIN WATER AND KATHY WILL GET DEHYDRATED EVEN THOUGH YOU ARE PUTTING FLUIDS IN.

[sun drawing] ON A HOT DRY FLUID NEEDS INCREASING 50% TO KEEP ELECTROLYTE LEVELS UP. THIS EXTRA 500 ML SHOULD BE DIORALYTE.

[ALWAYS] ENTER FLUID AMOUNTS IN THE RIGHT HAND COLUMN ON THE DIARY PAGE.　　200 ml　　150 ml

CHECK WHEN YOU COME ON SHIFT TO SEE IF KATHY NEEDS "TOPPING UP".

[IF YOU GO OUT] ALWAYS TAKE A SYRINGE AND A DRINK. (THERE IS A GROUND GLASS BOTTLE IN KATHY'S MEDICATION CUPBOARD WHICH CARRIES 200 ML.)

IF KATHY IS VOMITING / RETCHING - REDUCE AMOUNTS OF FLUID GIVEN AT ONE TIME BUT GIVE MORE FREQUENTLY EG INSTEAD OF 200 ML AT ONCE, GIVE 50 ML EACH ½ HOUR. IF IN DOUBT, GIVE DIORALYTE. IF VOMITING CONTINUES AFTER DOING THIS, CALL THE DOCTOR.

	NORMAL DAY	HOT DAY	
BREAKFAST	200 ml	150 ml	200 ml
MID-MORNING		100 ml	200 ml
LUNCH	200 ml	200 ml	100 ml
MID-AFTERNOON	100 ml		100 ml
TEA TIME	200 ml	200 ml	
MID-EVENING	100 ml		
BED TIME	200 ml	150 ml	150 ml
	1000 ml	1500 ml	
	1 LITRE	1½ LITRES	

THIS IS NOT A RIGID PATTERN BUT IS ILLUSTRATES HOW THE FLUID INTAKE MAY BE MANAGED. DETAILS WILL VARY ACCORDING TO WHAT YOU ARE DOING EG GOING SWIMMING, CLUB, STAYING HOME. THE IMPORTANT THING IS TO MAINTAIN THE TOTAL INTAKE AND SPREAD REASONABLY.

Sometimes Kathy's bottom got very sore and special arrangements were needed to prevent it breaking down any further. When several carers and different establishments were involved, it was important to give full details of what was required to avoid misunderstandings. An example of such an information sheet is below:

CARE OF KATHY'S NAPPY AREA

Changing Kathy's nappy:

Check frequently to see if it needs changing; this can be done discreetly. Sometimes she needs changing after 10 or 15 minutes; sometimes she will stay dry for several hours. Her nappy should be changed even if it is only wet.

Thorough cleaning is essential, even if only wet:

a. Wipe with soft paper if soiled

b. Wash with clean cotton wool and plain water

c. Dry thoroughly and gently

d. Apply cream (Nystan to vulva 3 times a day) Vasogen to bottom. Metanium if sore. Bottom must be creamed after each change.

e. Pay special attention to the cracks between Kathy's thighs and the spinal area above her anus; these crack easily.

NEVER use disinfectants, antiseptics (liquids or creams) on Kathy's bottom or in her washing water.

ALWAYS check Kathy's nappy last thing before you go to bed.

When Kathy moved into her independent living accommodation, I realised that staff needed some guidelines to help them get started about routines, at a fairly basic level. In a residential unit there is already some structure to the day and usually other staff around to check things with. In Kathy's new situation one member of staff would be working with her; the other member of staff would be working with her friend, and they might not even be in the bungalow. At this time Kathy had become increasingly fragile and was often unwell and/or uncomfortable, so routines had to be flexible. So I drew up the following notes:

KATHY SIROCKIN – DAILY CARE ROUTINES

DURING THE NIGHT

Clean and change nappy IF Kathy wakes.

MORNING

Remove soiled nappy and clean Kathy

N.B. Handle very slowly and carefully if she is stiff/distressed.

Place bed pad underneath and one on top to protect duvet. Give her dolls and books.

Put music on.

Give breakfast in bed – 1 slice bread broken into small pieces and mixed with one soft boiled egg chopped up. Offer drink – Formula-S Soya made to directions on tin; half boiling water, half cold water gives correct temperature.

Check pads periodically, change as necessary.

Give medication, giving soya with NGT if she has refused drink.

If giving medication in one go, give 200 ml soya. If you split medication because she is exceptionally loose, or retching, or indicating to you to stop tube feeding – you can give 150 ml soya with each portion of medication. (At least 30 minutes between each tube feed.)

Leave to rest for 20–30 minutes after medication.

Check pad periodically.

Run bath, get everything you need ready in bathroom. YOU CANNOT LEAVE KATHY ONCE SHE IS IN BATH.

Take Kathy to bathroom in wheelchair on a pad.

Lift into bath with hoist.

Clean teeth first, then face, then body.

Wash hair if necessary.

Check ears and clean.

Wrap in towels and return to bedroom.

Check for any bruises – use Arnica cream.

Check feet especially between toes for fungal infection.

Check condition of vulva and anal area.

Cream face (pot of face moisturiser) then apply Uvistat sun screen from April to October, and on bright winter days.

Cream body (bottle or tube of moisturising lotion); Uvistat on hands. If lightly clothed, Uvistat on hands and arms too.

Do physio routines while creaming.

Apply Canestan/Nystan to vulva.

Apply Metanium/Vasogen cream to anal area; make sure to cover pressure sore scars.

Dress appropriately to weather and occasion.

Put on splints and boots.

Comb hair.

Put Kathy in wheelchair and take her through to lounge/kitchen. Unless she is waiting for a brief period, or socialising round the table, she prefers to be on the floor.

Check wheelchair bag is complete:

> Spare nappy
>
> Spare bib
>
> Taxi card
>
> Tissues
>
> Info sheet pack
>
> Uvistat

If you are going out for several hours – hospital appointment or day out – add the following:

> wipes
>
> 2 syringes
>
> bottle of drink
>
> aspirins
>
> stripey bag with change of clothes

DURING THE DAY check nappy, clean, cream and change as necessary. Wipe face and hands, re-cream after meals, change clothes and bibs as necessary.

OUTINGS Check clothes suitable for weather, i.e. hat and mitts if cold. Waterproof if wet. Check wheelchair bags – see above. When lightly clothed carry jumper/top in bag.

BEDTIME Put Kathy in bed, check nappy, change into pyjamas. Give dolls. Clean teeth and wipe face and hands, cream. Give medication and 200 ml camomile. Don't change nappy for at least 30 minutes. Put night splints on – white, hard plastic.

I put these notes together by writing down what we did, and used notes some carers had made for themselves to remind them of routines. Once carers got to know Kathy they did not need such a basic list, but it was useful for new staff and for occasions when agency staff had to be used.

FURTHER INFORMATION

British Epilepsy Association, Anstey House, 40 Hanover Square, Leeds LS3 1BE. Tel: 0532–439393. Helpline: 0345-089599.

Epilepsy Federation, Stanley Mews, 71 Stanley Road, Thornton Heath, Surrey, CR0 3QF. Tel: 081–665–1255.

National Society for Epilepsy, Chalfont Centre, Chalfont St. Peter, Gerrards Cross, Bucks, SL9 0RJ. Tel: 0494–873991.

CHAPTER 9

MEDICATION

People with multiple disabilities often take some form of medication. It may be an anti-convulsant to control epilepsy, or medication to deal with a condition arising from the disability, such as drugs to relieve inflammation and pain in, say, rheumatoid arthritis. Some people like Kathy take many different drugs, added to over the years as further complications arise.

We asked the purpose of her various drugs as they were prescribed, and learned of their possible side effects. We also learned that some drugs 'interact' with others, that is, can make a drug work less effectively, or strengthen its effects. Sometimes these side effects and interactions can be dangerous. We began to ask doctors for these details as a routine whenever Kathy was prescribed a new drug. We also checked for more detail in the British National Formulary, which is used by doctors themselves for checking details when prescribing. You can buy this in bookshops that sell academic books, or get any bookshop to order it for you; you can also find it in the reference department of your local library.

We began to make a note of any side effects or interactions we noticed with Kathy. If she had recently been prescribed a new drug we would go back to the doctor or consultant and discuss the problem. We noticed, for example, that any drugs containing codeine or morphine seemed to make Kathy very agitated.

Similarly, occasionally when she was ill in hospital and very agitated she had been prescribed chlorpromazine, often known as Largactil, a strong tranquilliser. We found this made her more agitated, not less, and when we found out its other possible side effects such as sun sensitivity we insisted that from then on it was not prescribed for her.

It is important for carers to check these things. Some people with multiple disabilities are on a unique combination of drugs, and doctors are not always familiar with the possibilities of interactions. In Chapter 18 '*In Hospital*' I mention a potentially serious interaction Kathy experienced between one of her anti-convulsants and an anti-biotic. With some drugs, regular checks such as a blood test are needed to make sure serious side effects are not developing.

It is useful to keep and up-date a list of medication, with names of items, dosage amounts and times, details of any medication to be given only in special circumstances, and so on. This can then be used:

1. As a check-list for re-ordering supplies

2. To ensure accurate information is given to new doctors, other establishments, and in an emergency.

This was the layout for Kathy's medication list:

Katherine Sirockin (d.o.b. 17/11/63)
Drugs and Medical Requirements

DRUGS: MONTHLY

Epilim Syrup	200mg in 5ml	1200 ml
Tegretol Suspension	100mg in 5ml	900 ml
Ketovite Liquid	5ml spoon	150 ml
Prednisol	5mg	100 tabs
Ketovite Tabs		90 tabs
Sol Aspirin	300mg	240 tabs
Azathioprine	50mg	30 tabs
Clobazam	10ml	30 capsules

Stesolid Valium	5mg
	for rectal use in severe fits

CREAMS

Vasogen	6 tubes p.m. (nappy rash)
Canestan	4 tubes p.m. (thrush)
Metanium	2 tubes p.m. (severe nappy rash)

SUNSCREENS

Uvistat sun block   1 tube p.m. (2 in summer)

DIETARY

Cow and Gate formula
  S Soya   12 tins p.m.
                                     (other brands not well tolerated)

OTHER

Johnsons Blue Litmus
  Test Paper   1 pack p.m.

KY Jelly   1 tube as needed

Waterproof plaster:
  Sleek, setonplast, etc.

Supplied by X......... Hospital

Portex Naso-Gastric tubes Size 10FG Luer fitting

Order number 400/220/100 (contact Mr Z, Stores,
  081–000–1111 9 a.m. to 3 p.m Extn. 2345)

20 ml Disposable syringes (Order as above, boxes of 50)

JANUARY 199_

We used this list to re-order prescriptions once a month from our GP. We had to order the tubes and syringes direct from the hospital, so we kept a note of the arrangements for doing that. We had a lot of problems at first in obtaining regular supplies of tubes and syringes. Eventually they set up a shelf with her name on it in the hospital stores so there was always a spare box of each.

We carried the list at all times, even on outings. You may need it in unforeseen circumstances. If, for example, we had been out on a day trip, Kathy had experienced repeated and prolonged fitting on the journey home, and she had not responded to our usual treatment with rectal valium, we might call in at the first available hospital. We would be tired and anxious, and it was much easier to show a list of medication to a doctor than to try and remember details when we were under stress.

We tried various ways of noting dosages for Kathy's medication, to remind us and other carers. Residential units will have their own procedures and it is just a matter of giving them the accurate information. The list below was a simple reminder, giving the measures in ml. for the syrups and the quantities of tablets:

Katherine Sirockin		Drugs as at Sept 199_		
	A.M	*Lunch*	*Tea*	*Supper*
Epilim syrup	12.5	–	12.5	17.5
Tegretol syrup	10	–	10	10
Ketovite liquid	5	–	–	–
Ketovite tabs	1	–	1	1
Sol Aspirin 300mg tabs	2	2	2	2
Prednisol 5mg	2	–	1	–
Azathioprine 50mg	$\frac{1}{2}$ tab	–	$\frac{1}{2}$	–
Frisium 10mg capsule	–	–	–	1

In residential establishments all medication should be kept in a locked cupboard. At home or in a more informal caring setting such as a foster home this may not be felt necessary. It is important to remember that many of these drugs can be dangerous, even fatal, to others, especially small children, and storage should be secure from access by them or anyone else who is not authorised. Some medication needs to be kept in a refrigerator and a lockable one may be necessary for this purpose. We found out that some anti-biotics, the Ketovite liquid (a vitamin supplement) and the rectal valium tubes should all be kept in the refrigerator.

We always measured out Kathy's drug dosages separately, crushing or dissolving tablets and mixing them with a small amount of water, measuring syrups into separate graduated plastic containers. Then if we dropped or spilt any, or she sent any of them flying, we could usually work out which needed to be replaced. We encouraged carers to follow this system. There are details and photographs in Chapter 6, *The Care Book*.

If Kathy vomited while we were giving drugs, which happened at times, especially when she was unwell, we had been advised by doctors and nurses never to attempt to replace them. You could never be sure what had been absorbed and she might receive an overdose.

It is essential that carers record when medication was given, especially if there is to be a change of shift, or a change from home to another carer. Some residential establishments keep a chart for such purposes; in addition, we always asked for administration of any drugs to be recorded in the diary.

If temporary medication such as, an antibiotic, is prescribed, 'post-its' are useful to attach details temporarily to the list, as below:

> Ciproxin 250 mg.
>
> 2 tablets twice a day
>
> breakfast and teatime
>
> Started 10.6.90
>
> Course finishes 16.6.90
>
> For Kathy's Chest Infection

It is also very useful to have a brief summary letter signed by the GP or consultant, giving brief details of the disabilities/illnesses. This can be carried regularly and given to doctors when going to casualty unexpectedly or seeing a doctor when away from home. Kathy's consultant gave us the following letter to use:

> *X. Hospital.*
>
> *To whom it may concern.*
>
> *Re: Katherine Sirockin – d.o.b. 17.11.63.*
> *(Address)*
>
> *This patient suffers from mental retardation and cerebral palsy, inflammatory bowel disease, rheumatoid arthritis and epilepsy. Her General Practitioner is Dr. A, of (address and telephone number.) I have undertaken her hospital care.*
>
> *Should she require emergency care she should be taken either to P------- or Q------- hospital.*
>
> *Dr. Y-------.*

If you go abroad it is useful to have a letter from the GP or consultant giving details of medication and medical items you need to take. This is particularly important if you need to carry supplies of items such as syringes, especially if you need to carry needles. This is dealt with more fully in Chapter 20, Leisure Activities, where there is an example of such a letter.

Carers often asked us what Kathy's various drugs were for, and we included notes about this in her care book:

KATHY'S MEDICATION AND ITS PURPOSE

Epilim	To control fits (anti-convulsant)
Tegretol	As above
Clobazam	To control floppy fits
Prednisolone	To relieve inflammation and pain in the joints and bowel
Ketovite liquid	Fat soluble vitamin supplement
Ketovite tablets	Water soluble vitamin supplement

HYGIENE

It is important to keep bottles, spoons and pots clean. We always wiped the necks of bottles with kitchen roll after measuring out, to stop an accumulation of gunge around the neck and in the cap. We washed spoons, pots and so forth, thoroughly in washing up liquid and rinsed in hot water, draining on an ordinary kitchen drainer. We did re-use disposable syringes a few times and cleaned them in the same way, using the plunger to squish warm water through and rinsing thoroughly. We did not feel it necessary to take any other precautions. In one of Kathy's residential establishments they kept pots, syringes and so forth, in a Milton solution as they were concerned about maintaining adequate hygiene in a communal kitchen.

FURTHER INFORMATION

British National Formulary. Published by the British Medical Association and The Pharmaceutical Press. New editions frequently to keep up with changes. It gives full details of drugs, side effects and interactions. You can order it from any bookshop or direct from the British Medical Association, Tavistock Square, London WC1H 9JP.

Part Four

My Changing Needs

CHAPTER 10

IN NURSERY, SCHOOL OR CENTRE

A friend took her young son with severe intellectual disabilities to the local special school to look at the nursery. She had gradually come to terms with her own son's disability, but she came away very distressed. She had seen her own son as an individual, loved and valued in the family. For the first time she saw a group of older children with intellectual disabilities, some not as good looking or as advanced as her boy. She realised he was now in a 'category'. She also saw the future – she saw teenagers and said she worried that, however hard they all worked, and however successful his education was, he would still be seen by many people as in that 'category'.

I had a different lesson. As a single parent until Kathy was six, I worked. Kathy went to a local day nursery. I was asked to find alternative provision when she was three, as they could not cope with her screaming attacks. She was very fortunate to be able to go to the nursery run by the local MENCAP. When Kathy was five years old it was time to look for the next move. At that time there were no schools for children with 'severe mental handicap'. It was not until the 1970 Education Act that these children were brought within the school system in Britain.

Kathy was therefore seen by the local community physician, who came to our flat and gave her intelligence tests. I had been told this would happen and I tried to prepare Kathy for it. She spent most of her time playing on the floor, still very solitary, accepting one of us playing alongside her but not really wanting to play with us. She hated sitting, and it was very difficult to get her to stay in one place for even a few minutes. She spent most of her time juggling her favourite toys or crawling over the floor pushing little groups of these toys in front of her. I bought a small table and two chairs, and each day got her brother to sit on one, put Kathy on the other, and kneeling down to be at the same height, tried to involve her in simple play activities. She lasted only a few seconds the first time, but gradually began to sit still for a few minutes if the toys on the table were to her liking. By this time she would also stay still briefly if you sang to her, so Peter and I would do this to encourage her to sit a little longer.

The great day came. When the doctor arrived, I sat Kathy at her table. She was given some boards with different shapes fitted in; the doctor took the shapes out and asked Kathy to put them back in the right places. Kathy picked up the shapes, juggled them, then slipped off her chair and chased them round the room. I put her back on her chair, we picked up all the bits, and this time the doctor showed Kathy how to fit the pieces in. Kathy picked up the board, tipped it up so all the pieces fell out, and repeated her chasing routine. So it went on – the small doll was supposed to go in the bath, then on the chair, then in the bed; dolls and furniture ended up in a heap, chased around the room. Kathy did slightly better with the push toys as her brother played with these with her; she did push them, and she pushed a friction drive car properly. I was very proud of her when she lifted up a cloth to find the object underneath; we had been playing this game for weeks! I forget all the other tests; it all went on for about an hour. At the end the doctor was very kind and said we would get the results in a week or two. I asked her how Kathy had done. She replied that these tests were not very reliable with the lower ranges of ability, but when I pressed her she said Kathy had demonstrated an IQ (intelligence quotient) of 33. (The average person has an IQ of 100.)

In due course a letter arrived which told me that Kathy was 'ineducable'. I asked what facilities there were for her now she was five, and was offered a visit to the local 'junior training centre', which was the provision for five-to sixteen-year-olds who would later go on to the adult training centre. I spent the day there, during which I was treated as a person with learning difficulties by some of the staff. I discovered that most of the staff were unqualified. Children did not seem to be treated with respect; one member of staff pulled up a girl's dress and pulled down her knickers, in the girl's classroom, in front of the rest of the pupils to show me a rash which she said was due to parental neglect of her incontinence. A music lesson seemed to be an excuse for the member of staff to demonstrate his own tasteless sense of humour. I felt that staff were making an effort to provide a caring atmosphere in the special care unit, where Kathy would go along with anyone who had additional physical disabilities, but the educational content in the class seemed to be nil. I decided Kathy would not go there and asked the nursery to keep her on for a while, which they did.

HOME OR NURSERY?

Things have certainly moved on from the situation I have described. But it is still hard work to get the provision you feel is right for your child, at the right time. The early years are even more important for development with a child who has disabilities. Learning will need to be structured more carefully; she may not learn just by doing things and playing. If you prefer to keep your child at home during the day while she is very small, many areas now have a Portage scheme, named after the American town where it began. A trained Portage adviser will visit you at home and discuss with you what your child can do. Together you agree on activities and play which will build on what your child is able to do and encourage development. Parents and any other carers are fully involved in putting together and reviewing the programme, so activities can be changed as your child progresses. You can often borrow toys to give variety to play, and there may be a parents' group where you can share ideas and experiences.

By the time your child is two you may feel they need to mix with others. You may also feel you need a break during the day. You may have other children who need attention; you might want to catch up on household chores; you may have to go out to work; you might just need to rest. Small children with special needs are increasingly accepted, at least for trial periods, in ordinary nurseries. If your child has profound intellectual and multiple disabilities, she is likely to require a level of care and physical facilities which may not be available. Private nurseries and local play groups may be willing to give it a try; sometimes it works if the parent goes along to make the extra input, but that means you cannot do other things during that time, and it also means the child is not gaining any independence from you. Many special schools have nurseries, so children can attend full time from the age of two if that seems best. These nurseries are geared to young children with special needs but some do integrate with a wider range of children. You can ask for your child to go to one of these – you may arrange it yourself by contacting social services or the education department; they will arrange for you to visit the school. You can spend a day at the nursery to get the feel of the place. While your child is there you can ask for an assessment to be carried out, leading to a Statement of Special Educational Needs. You should play a full part in this process. (There is more about this later in this chapter.)

The nursery will have its systems for involving and communicating with parents. Ask what these are when your child starts there. Find out when you are welcome to go in. Get to know your child's classteacher and the classroom assistants. Join any parents' group; go to school activities – end of term plays and concerts, barbecues, social evenings. You will meet other parents, share experiences, make friends, and find out how to go about things if you are not entirely happy with the provision your child is receiving. A nursery attached to a special school will have arrangements for physiotherapy input and any other therapy required; private nurseries and playgroups are unlikely to have such arrangements.

AT SCHOOL

Before your child is five there should be a decision about the best next move – a special school, a unit attached to a mainstream school, and so on. You may want to consider a boarding school at some stage. (There is information at the end of the chapter on finding out about different types of school.)

Your child with profound intellectual and multiple disabilities is almost certainly going to be attending a special school or unit. A boarding school may, at some stage, be something you want to consider because of family needs, the nature of the disabilities, or some other reason. Some boarding schools are run by local authorities or other funding arrangements within the state system. Voluntary organisations run some catering for particular disabilities, particularly hearing and visual impairment. There are independent (private) schools which take children with special needs. Many of these specialist residential schools are increasingly prepared to take children with profound intellectual and multiple disabilities, as pupils with less severe or complex disabilities are now more likely to be integrated into mainstream schools.

While your child is being assessed, the local authority must inform the parents of the names of schools, including independent or non-maintained special schools, which may be suitable. If your child was given a Statement before the age of five, make sure you ask for this information when you need it.

If you are considering boarding school, you need to check what the arrangements for payment of fees are, whether the local authority will fund the place, and if you will be liable to contribute. Local authorities will fund places in independent (private) schools if that is the only suitable placement for a child, but it can be hard battle to get them to agree to this. If you can get a particular school that you feel is right for your child specified in the Statement, then the local authority must provide it.

Historically, special schools and mainstream schools have usually been built on separate sites, often far apart, making co-operation difficult. There are some mainstream schools which have units on site for children with disabilities. This provides the opportunity for social integration, especially at meal and play times, and there will be some opportunities for integrating in lessons.

You need to be realistic about education. When the National Curriculum was first introduced it had the effect of marginalising children with learning disabilities; those who drew it up obviously did not realise that children like ours existed. When it first became operative, one special school teacher said to me, 'I've read all the ring binders, I know what we are supposed to be doing. Where do I start? Most of the children in my class don't even make eye contact.' Children start working towards Level One when they start school at the age of five, and are expected to make steady progress, so that the average child will reach Level Seven by the time they are sixteen, with opportunities for the more able to reach up to Level Ten. Children with profound intellectual and multiple disabilities are said to be 'working within Level One'. This could seem depressing and pointless, but there are positive aspects:

1. The National Curriculum is only part of the curriculum offered to your child. There will be time for her to do things she enjoys – maybe painting, music, clay work, drama. The teacher will also be building in work on skills such as feeding or communication, and generally helping her to develop as much independence as possible.

2. Special school teachers have been working to find ways in which they can develop suitable work based on the National Curriculum. Just as the 1970 Education Act was a landmark in offering education for the first time to those with 'severe mental handicap', so the 1988 Education Reform Act offered new rights to children with profound intellectual and multiple disabilities, giving them an 'entitlement' to be taught the same subjects as other children. The challenge for schools and teachers has been to find sensible ways of introducing subjects such as science and history in a way that means something to children with this degree of disability.

3. Many of those involved with special schools have welcomed the chance to look afresh at the curriculum that is offered, to check whether the pupils are being offered too boring an experience with too much emphasis on routine 'skills'.

4. Even though, realistically, most children with profound intellectual and multiple disabilities will be 'working within Level One' for their entire school career, this does not mean they have to go on repeating the same thing year after year. Schools will need to provide a variety

of experiences as pupils go through the school, even if the aim is often to have another go at getting the same basic idea across.

As a parent or carer, you will want to be fully involved in your child's school experience. You can check how things are going in the following ways:

1. Get to know your child's class teacher, and ask how they go about things. Share your view of priorities for your child at a particular stage, and let the school know at once if you are concerned about anything that has happened, or any changes in your child that you think may be connected with school. Don't just accept suggestions made to you about things such as feeding programmes or physiotherapy routines; think how realistic these are in your particular family situation, and let the school know your views. For example, the school may suggest a feeding programme which is fine for them, but is difficult for you to carry out at home where you feel that it is important for all the family to eat together. You have to try and decide together which is more important.

2. Your child will almost certainly have a Statement of Special Educational Needs, and this will be reviewed once a year. Ask the school about the arrangements for this, and how you will be involved. You have a right to give information and suggestions for the review, and to be invited to the review meeting. The aim of the annual review is to discuss your child's progress over the last year, and to make any changes necessary to improve their chance of development. It must also consider whether your child's needs have changed and, if so, what needs to be done about this. When parents and carers are present at this discussion along with teachers and other professionals involved with the child, all aspects of the child's life can be considered, and there is more chance of everyone agreeing to work together consistently to bring about certain developments. Professionals need to know when they make suggestions how realistic these are in the home situation, and parents need to tell them.

3. Continue to get involved with school activities and with other parents; you will get most of your practical advice from others in the same situation.

4. Schools have parent representatives on the Governing Body. Find out who they are and talk to them about what you feel may need improving. You might like to become a Parent Governor yourself; you will certainly find out a lot about how the school works; you will be

involved in staff appointments, and you will find out about the pressures from the local authority and the Department For Education.

WHAT NEXT?

Children with special needs have the right to stay in education until they are aged nineteen. This should be discussed at the first annual review after your child is fourteen. Raise it again at the next annual review after that. If you want your child to stay on at school it is a good idea to write to the Head Teacher a year before she is sixteen; something on these lines would do:

The Headteacher,
Summerfield School

Dear Ms MacDonald,

Anita Henry
Mr Brown's class

As you know, Anita will be sixteen next July. I am pleased with her progress and she enjoys school. I would like her to stay on until she is nineteen.

Please let me know that this will be possible. I would also be interested to know whether she will stay in Mr Brown's class, or whether there will be some other arrangements for the older pupils.

I look forward to hearing from you,

Yours sincerely,

Some children with profound intellectual and multiple disabilities experience segregation even within the special school. Most schools are now moving away from keeping them all together in a special class. Kathy was in the same class with others like her at her last special school, from the age of fourteen until she left at nineteen. If this is the case in your school, ask what arrangements there will be for more integration from the age of sixteen. Many special schools have a leavers' unit for pupils aged sixteen to nineteen; find out if this is integrated, and if not, what the programme will be for your child.

For many carers, these last three years at school are often an anxious time, because of the patchy service for people with profound intellectual and multiple disabilities from the age of nineteen. Do not wait until the last year. Ask at the school what the options are in your area, and make sure that at each annual review this issue is discussed. Ask for health and social services to be represented at each review. Get in touch with other parents in a similar situation at the school. Ask your local MENCAP group or other voluntary organisation to take the issue up. Contact your local councillors; ask for meetings with the Chair of Social Services. When the economy is in trouble, adults with learning disabilities are an easy target for spending cuts, as local authorities are not legally obliged to provide day care.

You may ask for an assessment of needs under the 1989 Children Act up to the age of 18. This can cover all aspects of future needs of the person you care for, including education and day care. (There are more details about this at the end of Chapter 11, *Respite and Residential Services*.)

It is the experience of most parents, carers and teachers of young people with profound intellectual and multiple disabilities that they are often poised on the brink of significant developments in communication and other skills in their late teens. It is tragic that this is precisely the point at which they may be deprived of further opportunities for education and development.

There are further issues too. As the young person has reached the age of nineteen, she has usually grown much bigger and heavier. At the same time parents are getting older and finding care tasks more demanding – back troubles develop, arthritis makes some tasks more difficult, they get more tired. They need a guaranteed break during the day. The young person needs a break. They probably want to spend more time with people their own age, and staff and volunteers who will often have more in common with their interests than do parents. Kathy loved to be home with us, but not all the time; she got bored with just our company, all day and every day. Parents may be working, or may wish to work now; they cannot do this unless they have guaranteed arrangements for day provision. In addition to all this, day provision is not just about care. Continuing education is vital if the young person with profound intellectual and multiple disabilities is to continue developing skills and interests.

WHAT ARE THE OPTIONS?

1. Adult Training Centres, now often called Social Education Centres.

These are not always, or may say they are not, staffed or resourced to take people with profound intellectual and multiple disabilities. Kathy did attend a training centre. Physical facilities were accessible, but staffing was often stretched very thin and staff were understandably apprehensive about meeting all her needs. We met and prepared very carefully. We and her other carers visited the centre periodically to meet staff and see what kind of activities Kathy took part in. Staff were not permitted to give her tube feeds, so it was arranged that a community nurse came in at lunchtime to give her medication and fluids. The special diet caused some problems, so she usually took a packed lunch. Kathy was not able to join in all the activities, but she sometimes liked watching other people. She did enjoy and participate in the weekly music session. We took in some of her favourite things so that she could use them in some of the sessions. We discussed the things she liked doing and staff responded by trying to arrange them – going round the shops, lying outside on a rug in good weather, going swimming.

There were some problems with transport, because she was in a residential unit in a different borough. The benefits outweighed the problems, and staff became very confident with her. Kathy made friends with another student at the centre, an older man who was mobile. He met her each day and saw to her coat and other things. He joined her in some activities, and sat with her at breaks and lunch. When she was unhappy he would sit and comfort her; she would steal his chips and sausages if she got a chance. The relationship was good for both of them.

We met periodically with staff to discuss a common approach to Kathy's further development, and felt she benefited from the daily journey, the change of atmosphere, and the challenge of developing relationships with a wider group.

You should make sure that a personal programme is drawn up for the person attending the ATC/SEC; ask about arrangements for reviews and case conferences. Make sure that you attend, and that your interpretation of the needs of the person you care for is taken into account. If you are not happy with some aspects of the provision and have tried to change things through the procedures just described, you can ask the local authority to carry out a partial review of day services under Section 47 of the 1990 NHS and Community Care Act.

2. Outreach Services

Over the last thirty years, while more and more people with learning disabilities have left or never used the long-stay hospitals, local authorities have failed to expand adult training centre places or alternative forms of provision to cope with the increasing numbers leaving special schools locally and remaining within the community. Some authorities, faced with such large numbers that they have closed waiting lists, are reducing the number of days per week each person attends, and diverting some of the staff to 'outreach' work, to offer a service to some of the many who, from nineteen, are simply stuck at home, with the idea of using ordinary local facilities. While in principle most of us would agree that we would like all those with profound intellectual and multiple disabilities to be able to use such facilities, there are many practical obstacles. The outreach can be spread so thinly that it offers no more than a few hours a week of staff time. Even then, arrangements can break down because staff are over-stretched, local facilities are not accessible or have themselves closed because of cuts, or most likely of all, transport cannot be arranged.

3. Do-it-yourself

In some areas parents and or voluntary groups have set up imaginative schemes, obtaining funding from various sources, establishing a base, and using social work and other placements to provide extra staff input. An example of such a scheme is the Farnworth Special Needs Project in Bolton (details at the end of the chapter).

Some individual parents I know have successfully applied for funding from the local authority and from the Independent Living Fund to pay staff to organise day activities for their young adults without a day place. This makes it more likely that activities will meet the needs of the young person, gives the carer a break and gives the young adult some independence from the home. However, parents who are doing this say it is very hard work. You are employing your own staff, and need to get advice on this; the best way is to use an agency, then you do not need to be concerned about national insurance, employment legislation, and so on. The agency should check that the person has no criminal record and assess their general suitability to work with young people. Staff leave periodically, so you have to go through the process again and again. The carers have to do all the legwork to find out what facilities and activities may be available. Arrangements can fall through when a council funded activity is closed down, or when a class refuses to allow the young person to continue.

4. Further Education Colleges

There are some residential Further Education Colleges run by bodies such as MENCAP which offer courses for students with various disabilities, usually from the age of eighteen or nineteen. There should be more opportunities for students with learning disabilities in Further Education Colleges following the 1992 Further and Higher Education Act. This has changed the way colleges are funded, and under Schedule 2 of the Act they must consider the needs of students with learning disabilities when planning their courses. They must provide courses for all 16–18 year olds, and under certain conditions students with learning disabilities are now entitled to specialist provision up to the age of twenty-five.

A difficult choice? Yes, because a young person's Statement will not operate once they leave school. On the other hand, if you are planning ahead for several years, and suitable courses are available, there could be benefits for a young person in moving to a more adult environment and being stimulated by fresh challenges.

Day or boarding? Most local Further Education Colleges have little experience in providing appropriate courses for students with profound intellectual and multiple disabilities as yet, so if you are looking for local colleges, you will need to check this out thoroughly. You will also want to know if the support services provided at school are going to be available at college, for example:

- Transport
- Access to Physiotherapy
- Personal care facilities, eg. for incontinence
- Back-up for dealing with conditions such as epilepsy, diabetes
- Eating arrangements, eg. specialist equipment, feeding when needed
- Equipment for those with sensory disabilities.

Some of the independent colleges have more experience in this area. Again, you would need to check whether the courses are suitable for someone with profound intellectual and multiple disabilities, and whether the back-up services are sufficient. Most of the independent colleges are boarding, so unless you live very near, the person you care for will be away from home, at least during the week. This may be a very positive move if you and they are ready for it.

If you are applying on behalf of a student to an independent college, you will need to cover the following points:

1. Find out about and visit several colleges to decide the best provision.

2. Ask the local education authority to assess the student's needs.

3. Arrange for applications to colleges and attendance at interviews.

4. If the student is accepted, check what the local education authority is doing about funding.

5. If funding is not agreed, you will be told how to appeal.

6. If the student has been assessed and has a Care Plan under the 1990 NHS and Community Care Act, (see the next chapter), the local social services may pay part of the fees.

Lack of day provision can increase the burdens on carers to the point where they feel they can no longer cope. While it should be possible for the young person to have more independent living arrangements away from home, this should be a carefully planned and timed decision, if possible with the consent of all concerned. No one should be pushed into such decisions through intolerable pressures. It is very short-sighted for local authorities to fail to plan adequate day provision, because it will inevitably lead to a breakdown in care arrangements in some cases.

It is also wasteful to provide education up to the age of nineteen and then effectively cut the young disabled person off from any hope of further development.

STATEMENTS OF SPECIAL EDUCATIONAL NEEDS

The 1981 Education Act, re-enacted in the 1993 Education Act, provides for a local authority to carry out an assessment of your child and then issue a Statement which describes their special needs and says how and where they should be met. You, the authority or the school can ask for this to happen. If your child has profound intellectual and multiple disabilities, this will have become clear long before she is five years old. You can request a Statement to be drawn up when your child is two, or earlier if you feel you are not getting the services she needs. If you have a social worker they can help you to do this. You write to the local education authority making this request. If your child is in a nursery or school, they may also make the request; in this case, it is best to work together.

You will get information from the local authority about the stages of the assessment, and about your input and rights. You can get more details and advice about the whole process from ACE, CSIE, Contact a Family and IPSEA (the addresses are at the end of this chapter).

There is a Code of Practice setting out full details of how the procedure should be carried out. You can get a copy of this from the Department for Education (address at the end of the chapter).

Who does this assessment?

The local authority carries out the assessment. They should take information from everyone working with your child – teachers, doctors, educational psychologists, physiotherapists, speech therapists and, most important, parents and carers. You can check exactly how you should be involved by contacting one of the above organisations for advice.

While the assessment is going on, the local authority must give parents information about voluntary organisations, support groups and so forth which may be helpful for them and their child.

They must also give parents the name of the officer who will be dealing with the assessment. You can ask this person for further information and advice.

The local authority must make arrangements for translation and interpreters where the first language of the parents or carers is not English.

If the authority decide to go ahead with a Statement, they must give you a draft first. This must not name the school they might think is best, so that you have the opportunity to give your preference. You can get further advice at this point before the final Statement is issued.

Will this statement stigmatise my child?

Some parents feel strongly that they do not want their child labelled. They may feel that the Statement will do this. The problem is that the resources follow the Statement. If the child does not have one, she may not receive the appropriate resources for her development. It is perhaps more helpful to see the Statement as a chance to state accurately the needs of your child, so that she will receive the education and other resources she needs. If your child has profound intellectual and multiple disabilities, avoiding putting them down on paper will not make them go away.

How will the statement help my child?

1. The Statement should state your child's needs accurately; you need to play a full part in this process. It should then list the provision your child needs for her full development; you will need to check this yourself and take advice, as some Statements are deliberately vague about provision because of lack of resources. Provision includes physiotherapy and speech therapy as well as the straight educational resources. If you think a specific school is the right one for your child, get it named on the Statement, as then it must be provided.

2. Once the Statement is drawn up, your child has a legal right to the provision listed. You are on strong ground in challenging any gap.

3. The Statement provides for the child until she is nineteen if she stays at school.

4. There will be an annual review of your child's progress, where teachers and other professionals involved with her will meet together to discuss the past year, review her needs and set goals for the next year. Parents have a right to give their views and to be present at the review meeting. You can make suggestions to improve your child's development.

    The annual review is a valuable opportunity for people involved with different aspects of your child's care and development to meet and share views. The Statement can be amended during this annual review.

    If parents need arrangements such as an interpreter, translation of papers, alternative communication systems such as British Sign Language, information in braille or on tape, so they can take a full part in the review meeting, these must be provided.

5. At the first annual review after the young person's fourteenth birthday, representatives from social services, further education and careers service must be present. This review meeting should plan ahead for the rest of her time at school and afterwards. This is a good opportunity to make sure that all the possibilities for continuing education after school are explored, at an early stage. A Transition Plan must be prepared which will involve all those concerned with care and services in planning ahead for the young person's adult life.

    *   *Suppose the authority refuses to do an assessment?*
    *   *What if the authority refuses to issue a Statement?*

- *What can I do if I disagree with the Statement or some or all of the suggested provision?*

  Parents have their rights in these matters set out clearly in the Code of Practice. Your rights to appeal at various stages are also explained. Contact one of the organisations listed at the end of the chapter for advice.

- *What happens if I move to another area?*

  The Code of Practice will ensure that the new education authority will accept the Statement and you will not be asked to start all over again.

- *Are there any disadvantages?*

  1. As with all these procedures, it will make work for you. You may need help in making the written submissions. You will need to keep copies of everything you send in and keep to all the papers in order.

  2. It takes a long time. Some authorities are reluctant to issue statements because this legally binds them to make appropriate provision. They may try to put you off in various ways. The Code of Practice sets out time limits and guidelines for the process.

  3. Some authorities resist making the Statement very specific to avoid committing themselves to the necessary resources. You will need to be very specific about what you think is needed, and make sure at every stage that it does not get watered down.

  4. If a pupil goes to college rather than stays at school from sixteen years, the Statement will no longer apply. However, a copy of the Statement, the last annual review and the Transition Plan will be passed to the college unless the parents object.

FURTHER INFORMATION

ACE (Advisory Centre for Education), 1B Aberdeen Studios, 22–24 Highbury Grove, London N5 2EA. Telephone: 071–354–8321. Free guidance to parents. Publish an excellent guide to the 1981 Act 'ACE Special Education Handbook', updated to take account of the 1993 Education Act and Code of Practice.

Autistic Society, National, 276 Willesden Lane, London NW2 5RB.Tel: 081–451–1114. Details of schools on request.

Barnardo's, Tanners Lane, Barkingside, Ilford, Essex IG6 1QS. Tel: 081–550–8822. Information about schools for children with severe disabilities.

Blind and Physically Handicapped Jewish, Society for the, 118 Seymour Place, London W1 5DJ. Tel: 071–262–2003.

Blind, Royal National Institute for the, 224 Great Portland Street, London W1N 6AA. Tel: 071–388–1266. Educational Services, including advice, home visits, schools, colleges, etc.

Leonard Cheshire Foundation, Leonard Cheshire House, 26–29 Maunsel Street, London SW1P 2QN. Tel: 071–828–1822. Schools and homes for children and adults with any type of disability.

CSIE (The Centre for Studies on Integration in Education), 4th Floor, 415 Edgware Road, London NW2 6NB. Telephone: 081–452–8642. Produce free or cheap leaflets explaining in more detail about statementing and educational provision. Free advice service.

Children's Legal Centre, 20 Compton Terrace, London N1 2UN. Telephone: 071–359–9391. (2.00 to 5.00 p.m.) Free advice service.

Contact a Family, 170 Tottenham Court Road, London W1P 0HA. Tel: 071–383–3555. Information sheets and advice.

Deaf Children's Society, National, 45 Hereford Road, London W2 5AH. Tel: 071–229–9272. Parents' organisation – information and advice; register of all organisations concerned with hearing impairment.

Deaf, Royal National Institute for the, 105, Gower Street, London WC1E 6AH. Tel: 071–387–8033. Information about schools, etc.

Deaf, Scottish Association for the, Moray House, Holyrood Road, Edinburgh, EH8 8AQ. Tel: 031–557–0591. As above.

Department for Education, Special Education Division, Sanctuary Buildings, Great Smith Street, London SW1P 3BT. Telephone: 071–925–5000.

Farnworth Special Needs Project – day services for people with profound intellectual and multiple disabilities. Contact: Alice Crompton, tel. 0204–73107.

Independent Living (1993) Fund, P.O. Box 183, Nottingham NG8 3RD. Tel: 0602–290423 or –290427.

IPSEA (Independent Panel for Special Education Advice) 12 Marsh Road, Tillingham, Essex, CM0 7SZ. Telephone: 0621–779781. Advice on the assessment process and especially on appeals.

MENCAP, Education and Training, MENCAP National Centre, 123 Golden
  Lane, London EC1Y ORT. Tel: 071–454–0454.

MENCAP Profound Intellectual and Multiple Disabilities (PIMD) Section,
  Piper Hill School, 200 Yew Tree Lane, Northenden, Manchester M23 OFF.
  Tel: 061–998–4161. Co-ordinator: Helen Mount.

Portage Association, National, 127 Monk's Dale, Yeovil, Somerset, BA21 3JE.
  Tel: 0935–71641. Details of local schemes sent on request.

SENSE (National Deaf-Blind and Rubella Association), Head Office, 11–13
  Clifton Terrace, Finsbury Park, London N4 3SR. Tel: 071–272–7774.
  Information about schools; adult services in some regions.

Spastics Society, 12 Park Crescent, London W1N 4EQ. Helpline:
  0800–626216. Information about their own schools, education generally,
  many other services.

Voluntary Council for Disabled Children, 8 Wakley Street, London EC1V
  7QE. Telephone: 071–278–9441. Free information service.

Publications

'After 16 – What Next?' (published by SKILL: National Bureau for Students
  with Disabilities and the Family Fund. Available from the Family Fund, PO
  Box 50, York, YO1 2ZX. Tel: 0904–62 11 15.)

Code of Practice for Special Needs Sections of the 1993 Education Act and
  Guide for Parents. Available from May 1994, from the Department for
  Education, address above. Tel: 071–925–5000.

'16+ COPE Directory', Wiltshire Guidance Service, Support Services Unit,
  County Careers Centre, County Hall Annexe, Bythesea Road, Trowbridge,
  Wiltshire, BA14 8EZ.

'Directory of Opportunities for School Leavers'. (Published by Queen
  Elizabeth's Foundation for the Disabled, Leatherhead, Surrey, KT22 OBN.
  Tel: 0372–842204.)

'Learning for Life', a pack to support learning opportunities for adults who
  have profound intellectual and multiple disabilities. Available from
  MENCAP, address below.

'Ordinary Everyday Families' (Under Fives Project), MENCAP Bookshop, 123,
  Golden Lane, London EC1Y ORT. (Good on how assessment affects
  families, good ideas about organising things, parents' experiences – relevant
  for over-five's as the basic principles stay the same.)

'Portage- Pre-Schools, Parents and Professionals.' Cameron, D. (ed.) Windsor
  NFER-Nelson.

'Working Together – Portage in the UK.' Cameron, D. (ed.) Windsor NFER-Nelson.

Children with Special Needs: Assessment, Law and Practice – Caught in the Act, 2nd edition. Harry Chasty and John Friel. Jessica Kingsley Publishers. ISBN 1 85302 155 5

Young Adults with Special Needs: Assessment, Law and Practice – Caught in the Acts, John Friel. Jessica Kingsley Publishers. ISBN 1 85302 231 4.

CHAPTER 11

RESPITE AND RESIDENTIAL SERVICES

Some parents who learn at the birth of their baby that she has profound intellectual and multiple disabilities, feel unable to accept her and cannot bring themselves to take her home. She may then go into residential care or, increasingly often now, to a fostering placement. This decision must be influenced by the way in which parents learn about their baby's disabilities, what they are offered in the way of support, and their own previous knowledge and views about disabilities. Most take their baby home and are soon so busy getting through each day that they do not have time to worry about the long term.

However, it must be acknowledged that caring for any person with profound intellectual and multiple disabilities is very hard work. Parents may have to struggle to communicate, meet medical needs, deal with fits, feed a child where every meal may take two hours, go to frequent appointments, cope the next day after sleepless nights – and all the while there is the endless washing. Other children may feel neglected; partners will feel the strain; the health of the main carer will inevitably suffer. However much you love the person you care for, however responsive they are, however rewarded you are by each development, there will come a time when you must consider a break – for you and the rest of the family. It is amazing how long you seem able to cope, even without much sleep, as long as you keep going. Of course you cannot afford to have the 'flu or even think about yourself and your needs. In the long run, this is not good for anyone. Many parents feel so guilty about even thinking about a brief period of respite care that they go on for many years, until an illness or a brief period in hospital means that the person they care for has to go away for a while. Then they wonder how they ever managed without that break. It must be your decision if and when you seek such a break, but those supporting you professionally should give you all the information you need to make that decision.

RESPITE CARE

When Kathy was very young, I was offered two weeks' respite care each year. This would be in some institution on the outskirts of London. The social worker would take us by car or arrange transport. When we arrived, no one seemed to want much information about her and she was soon whisked off. When I telephoned to ask how she was, she was always fine. I never really knew how she got on during those times; she could not tell me and no one else did.

There are more possibilities nowadays. Many local authorities have their own respite care residential units, and you can plan for occasional or regular breaks. Some have arrangements with private or voluntary homes in or outside your area. There are some local schemes, often called 'shared care', where other parents will take your child for a temporary stay. Your social worker should give you details of any provision; if you do not have a a social worker, contact your local social services department for information. If they are not helpful, telephone the MENCAP or Spastics Society helplines (details at the end of this chapter). It is sometimes possible for the respite to be a proper holiday for your child, in the country or at the seaside, with planned activities. Unfortunately, when cutbacks are being made, respite care often suffers, and parents are offered less frequent breaks, or the more expensive provision, such as the holiday placements, is withdrawn.

Once you have been offered some form of respite care, you will want to consider the following:

1. Visit the place first, whether it is a unit or a private family home. Talk to the people who will care for your child; try to speak to the person in charge. Ask to look round. Insist on seeing where your child will sleep. Try to visit at a meal time, and look at the quality of the food. Ask how they will take information about your child's needs, including medication. Ask if she will wear her own clothes and if not, why not. If your child uses pads, ask whether you have to supply these. Explain about any special equipment your child uses.

2. Ask if your child can spend a few hours there during the day before staying overnight. This will help her to get to know people and become familiar with the new surroundings. Any problems that arise then can be discussed before a longer stay.

3. Talk to your child about respite care beforehand. She may not seem to understand, but she will be taking in some information, even if only that there will be some change. You may be able to find books with pictures that help you to explain what is happening. Pack any items

that will go with her while she is in the room, and talk to her about it. Keep talking her through it, especially when getting her up on the day she is to go and on the journey there.

4. Prepare information for those who will care for her. Care books, information sheets – anything that explains clearly what needs to be done to keep her happy, comfortable, well and safe.

5. Make sure personal items that are important to her go with her. If they are very precious to her, make sure staff realise this. Tell them what to do if things get soiled.

6. Take her diary when you go and explain how you want it completed.

7. Ask what they will do if your child is ill or there is an emergency. Make sure they have details of where to contact you. If you are going out for the day or away on holiday, give them full written details.

8. When you collect your child, ask to sit down with a member of staff, or the foster parent, and ask in detail how she has been. If you are worried about anything there and then – a bruise, the fact that she looks unhappy or pale, or some of her personal things are missing – say so. If your concern arises once you have gone home, get in touch at the earliest opportunity to speak about what is worrying you.

9. If you are not happy about the way a member of staff has spoken to you or your child, or about the way they have behaved, ask to speak to the person in charge. If your child was with a foster parent or a voluntary organisation, you may need to contact the local council or the person in charge of the scheme. If you have a social worker, they can do it for you.

10. If things went well, tell the staff or the foster parents. They like to feel they are doing a good job, and will be pleased to have this confirmed by the carer who knows the disabled person best. In a good respite care situation information on caring strategies can be two-way, so that you and respite staff can share ideas.

Do not feel guilty about asking for respite care. If you are going to go on and do a good caring job, you must look after yourself. This includes rest, breaks and holidays for you and other family members. As your child grows older, you may find they quite enjoy a break from you and the family too!

If you need more respite care than you are offered, say so. Point out that if you break down, social services will have to provide residential care.

Do not hesitate to raise any worries you have about anything that might have happened to your child while she was away from you. You are bound to worry when you read about cases of cruelty and abuse in residential establishments. If you have the slightest doubt, talk to someone in authority. Residential establishments should have a proper complaints procedure, and you should be told about it. If your child goes somewhere regularly, you will build up a relationship with care workers and will feel more able to trust them.

ADULT RESPITE CARE

Everything above applies. When the disabled person is older and bigger, carers need more support, and a break may be one of the answers. It is possible that the adult you care for may find ways of letting you know they do not want to go away for a while. You have to make the decision, because you have to deal with the consequences. In fact, many disabled adults welcome a change of surroundings and company.

If you are not receiving respite care services, would like to, or would like to increase the amount, ask your local authority to carry out an assessment of the care needs of the disabled person, under Section 47 of the 1990 NHS and Community Care Act. If you are caring for a child or young person up to the age of 18, their needs will be assessed under the 1989 Children Act. You are also entitled to ask for an assessment of your own ability to go on caring (Section 8 of the Disabled Persons Act 1986), as this is vital in deciding what services are needed. Once they have agreed respite care is needed, they must provide it. They will make a charge for adults, and may do so for children, but must still provide the service, even if you do not pay.

HOLIDAYS

I referred earlier in this chapter to holiday breaks for the person with disabilities. Many local authorities run or have run schemes whereby they fund a holiday, either at an establishment with which they have regular links, or at a private or voluntary holiday centre. Some will give grants for the disabled person to go on holiday with the family. In recent years this provision has often been reduced or cut altogether. Ask your local Social Services department for details of any schemes. Local charities sometimes fund holiday placements for disabled people. Your Social Services department will have details. You should also contact the MENCAP and Spastics Society helplines, especially if you are finding it difficult to get information.

Holiday breaks for disabled people come under the 1970 Chronically Sick and Disabled Persons' Act, and you can ask for the need to be assessed. (Details of organisations which arrange or have information about holidays are given at the end of Chapter 20, *Leisure*.)

CARE ATTENDANT SCHEMES

In recent years there has been a growth in the number of schemes to provide care support in the home of the person with the disabilities. You can request help at the 'crunch' times of getting up and bedtime, or whatever seems best to meet the needs of the disabled person and the carers. This support can make all the difference to carers being able to carry on; it is particularly valuable if carers are beginning to suffer from back strain or similar problems through constant lifting. You can request this help through Social Services. Someone will visit you and assess the needs. If you are given this support, ask about training for the carers, and ask to meet those who will work in your home before they actually start work. You will need to work alongside them the first few times to show them the best ways of managing. Then you may find they have useful ideas to share with you. (Details of schemes are at the end of the chapter.)

You may find the idea of having a stranger in your home, sharing the care and using your domestic facilities, difficult at first, especially if your home is not very large. The organisation arranging the care support should be sensitive to your wishes, and what you see as the needs and wishes of the person you care for. You may want the care worker to be from a particular ethnic group; you may want to specify that only a female worker will be acceptable. You will have to see how the care worker gets on with the person you care for, and you will have to develop a good working relationship. You will need to be very precise about arrangements, for instance the time you will return if you go out while the care support worker is in your home. You will need to think about how bathroom and toilet facilities are best managed, balancing the needs of all members of the family. Breakfast times will need planning and perhaps staggering if there are several people needing to go out to school or work. You may find that you need adaptations to your home to make the new arrangements work properly, and there is information about the possibilities for these in Chapter 14.

When Kathy started having care support workers we found it was like any partnership – there were difficulties and misunderstandings at times, and all parties had to work at it. We had to make Kathy's needs very clear, and discussion of procedures was based on that. Kathy got on better with some of her workers than with others, and developed warm and positive relation-ships with many. We tried to raise any disagreements directly with care workers first, and encouraged them to do the same with us. If things could not be sorted out at that stage, the employing agency had ways of managing discussions – sometimes a meeting was a good idea, with others present who were a little removed from the direct situation. As care support workers got to know Kathy, they often had useful and important ideas to improve her care and to make her life more interesting.

INDEPENDENT LIVING (1993) FUND

This is an agency handling government funds; money is allocated to people with disabilities for the costs of their personal and domestic care. You can apply on behalf of the disabled person or your social worker can help you. You get the application form from the local authority social services office or direct from ILF. (The address is at the end of the chapter.) The ILF information leaflet tells you who can apply:

Who Can Get Help?

An applicant to the Fund must meet *all* the following conditions:

1. be at least 16 and under 66 years of age,

2. receive the highest rate of the care component of Disability Living Allowance,

3. be at risk of entering residential care (or currently be in residential care and wish to leave and live independently),

4. live alone or with people who cannot fully meet the care needs,

5. be on Income Support or have an income above Income Support level which is less than the cost of care needed,

6. have savings of less than £8000.

Someone from the ILF will arrange to visit you at home with the local authority social worker. They will ask about the applicant's care needs, how care is being carried out at present, and what the applicant's financial circumstances are.

The local authority must be providing or agree to provide at least £200 worth of services a week; then the ILF will work out the amount the Fund will pay on top of this. They get in touch after this visit to tell you what help you can receive from the Fund. Once you know exactly how much money the disabled person will be receiving from the ILF each month you will need to make arrangements for opening an account to receive this payment, and engaging staff to do the agreed jobs. (There is more about this in the next chapter.)[1]

RESIDENTIAL OPTIONS

An adult with profound intellectual and multiple disabilities may want to leave home as much as any other person their age. Kathy loved to come home for weekends and longer periods, and enjoyed holidays with us. However, she liked the company of other young people, and she liked a change from us. We shared many tastes and interests, but there were different things she liked doing with other people. Parents and carers might also wish to give more time to others in the family, or indeed to themselves; they may need a rest from the physical demands of caring. Regular periods of respite care may meet all these needs for some time, if the arrangements are reliable and everyone is happy with them. However, there may come a time when full time residential care is needed, often with the arrangement for the disabled person to come home for periods if they wish and everyone can cope.

Some parents may have made this decision, as we did, at an earlier stage. They may find the demands of caring too difficult to balance with other needs in the family, and with their own needs and health. A marriage or relationship may have broken down. The needs of the disabled person may have intensified – perhaps a chronic disease developed on top of the disabilities; a brain tumour led to loss of sight and perhaps some skills; challenging behaviour became too much to manage in a small home; severe epilepsy led to loss of some skills and perhaps more difficult behaviour. The principal carer has to make the decision – they carry the day-to-day burden and responsibility. (There is more about making these difficult decisions in the Conclusion.) If you are caring for a child, you do not have to give up your parental rights if she goes into residential accommodation. You can retain full rights and make arrangements for visiting and taking her home for periods, working these out with the place where she goes.

Once the decision to seek residential care is made, the hard work begins. You may be having mixed feelings about all this, or you may be so ill and exhausted that you see no alternative. In any case, talk to the person you care

---

1   The Independent Living (1993) Fund was set up to replace the previous ILF arrangements. There is an ILF (Extension) Fund which continues payments only to clients entitled under the previous arrangements. There are some differences in the conditions and arrangements between the two funds. The ILF funding discussed in the next chapter was under the old arrangements.

for about your decision and try to involve them in all discussion and arrangements. If you have a social worker, they should be advising you. You can also get information from the MENCAP and Spastics Society helplines. These are the main options:

1. A Local Authority Residential Unit

Many local authorities run residential units for children and adults with disabilities. Some of these may not cater for people with profound intellectual and multiple disabilities – physical access may not be satisfactory; staffing levels may not be adequate to give proper care. There may be a waiting list. Ask what the criteria are for priority. If you are told the person you care for is too severely disabled for that unit, ask why. If it is a matter of staffing or making adaptations, ask why adjustments cannot be made. Once you are offered a place, ask to visit with the person you care for. You want to meet staff, and look at the arrangements. Ask if you can have a meal there. Arrange for the disabled person to spend a few hours there at first, to get used to people and the new surroundings. Take your Care Book, information sheets and anything else that will be needed by staff to give proper care.

Involve yourself in the life of the unit – join any carers' group, ask about planned activities and outings such as Bonfire Night, barbecues. If you want to celebrate a birthday at the unit rather than at home, discuss what special arrangements might be made. Everyone enjoys a treat and a change. We would talk to staff and agree who would organise the cake and food, who would be invited, and what form the celebrations would take. When Kathy was younger we would organise party games such as pass the parcel; sometimes friends would come in and play music. When she became a teenager, she liked her friends and workers to join her for a meal, and then have a disco to follow. Sometimes a group of us went out to a restaurant for a change.

You will need to develop a good working relationship with staff. Most residential establishments operate a key worker system, with one worker taking special responsibility for a particular resident. A development programme should be drawn up by all involved, so that the unit and other carers are working together to make the best use of the abilities of the disabled person. Try and raise any concerns with the member of staff involved directly. If you cannot sort it out at that level, ask to speak to the next in charge. The unit should have a formal complaints procedure if you have serious concerns. Do not hesitate to raise any anxieties you have. If your concerns prove to be unfounded, so much the better. If not, you will not forgive yourself for delaying. If you cannot seem to sort things out through the complaints procedure, do not hesitate to get in touch with your local councillor, who can intervene on your behalf. Once you have involved them, you can always go on to complain to the Local Government Ombudsman if necessary.

2. Private or Voluntary Homes

If the local authority does not have a suitable local unit, they can fund a place at a private or voluntary establishment. This may not be local. You can find a list of suitable establishments yourself. (See details at the end of the chapter.) Your social worker may also be able to help. You will want to visit any possible places. If you have no transport or cannot afford to do this, ask your social worker to make arrangements. Ask all the questions suggested above about local authority units. See if it is possible to be put in touch with other parents so you can ask them what they think. If it is a good establishment, they will not mind doing this. Ask the Registration Unit of the local authority in which the home is situated to arrange for you to see the annual reports. You may find you do not have much choice in finding suitable provision for the particular needs of the disabled person you care for. However, do bear in mind the problems of distance. When Kathy was cared for at a distance of more than a hundred miles from our home, visiting her was expensive and took time. It was also more difficult to sort out any difficulties at that distance. Getting in touch with local doctors and hospitals was more complicated. If it is the right placement, then it is worth it. If money is short, find out first what assistance you can expect with travelling to visit. Once you have found a suitable place, you will need to apply to the local authority to fund it. (See details on the 1990 NHS and Community Care Act at the end of the chapter.)

3. Fostering

Fostering placements are increasingly used now for people with profound intellectual and multiple disabilities, for respite and long term care, for both children and adults, the latter sometimes called Adult Care Schemes. Some local authorities operate special schemes, as do some voluntary and charitable organisations. Payment is made, and usually training and support is offered to the foster parents. Parents may have mixed feelings about fostering. They may feel that if they received more support they would be able to cope themselves. Establishing relationships between the natural and the foster family may be a delicate matter, especially if care is to be shared. Some foster parents take on children with disabilities who have been neglected or abused; if the natural parents have access, this may not be an easy relationship. Long term foster parents and those who adopt children with profound intellectual and multiple disabilities need to consider respite care for the same reasons as natural parents.

4. Independent Living Schemes

It is possible to arrange for a person with profound and multiple disabilities to live 'independently' even if they require twenty-four-hour care. The Spastics Society run some successful schemes. There are a number of projects in preparation, some of them by groups of families looking for a better quality of life for their sons and daughters. Kathy moved into her own council tenancy four months before her death, with a friend whose level of disability was similar. There was much detailed planning to do to get this off the ground. (The details are in the next chapter.)

5. NHS Units and Hospitals

Although many long-stay hospitals have closed, some still exist, although they often cater for smaller numbers of people. Some offer specialised provision for particular needs, for example severely challenging behaviour. Some units and hospitals continue to exist because, quite simply, there is no provision to replace them. If this is what you are offered, the first thing you need to establish is why this provision is considered suitable for the person for whom you care. Unless a hospital can offer quality care which meets the particular needs of the person for whom you care, and which can be provided nowhere else, you should ask for a more home-like residential unit. You can find out more about a particular hospital by contacting your own CHC (Community Health Council) and the CHC in the area of the hospital if that is different. They should know about parents' groups, visitor schemes, and so on, and you should speak to as many people as possible about the quality of care, as well as visiting. MENCAP will also be able to give you information. Benefit and financial arrangements are different from those for other forms of residential care. The *Disability Rights Handbook* gives more information. (Details at the end of the chapter.)

PAYMENT FOR RESIDENTIAL CARE

Benefit arrangements will change once a disabled person goes into residential accommodation. Their books will be handed over to the residential establishment, except for the mobility component of Disability Living Allowance. They will name an appointee who will handle the benefits on behalf of the disabled person. Most of the money from the benefits will go to pay the fees for residential accommodation; a weekly allowance is made for pocket money. (There is more about payment for residential care in Chapter 15 and at the end of this chapter, where the laws are explained briefly.) Financial arrangements for a disabled person who has an independent living scheme are different, and are explained in Chapter 12.

There are standard payments for respite care for adults which local authorities are obliged to charge. Some authorities make charges for respite care for children. Carers keep the benefit books during respite care, but the Disability Living Allowance Care Component may be affected – see Chapter 15.

COMMUNITY CARE – THE LAW AND YOUR RIGHTS

1970 Chronically Sick and Disabled Person Act: You can ask the local authority social services to assess the needs of a disabled person and their carers for a range of services, including help with caring, equipment, adaptations. If they agree you need the service/item, they must provide it. The problem may be getting them to agree to the need. Make sure the person you care for is registered as disabled with the local authority. There is now a procedure for complaining if your needs are not being met; see RADAR and Carers National Association leaflets (details at end of chapter.)

1986 Disabled Person's Act: This strengthens the 1970 Act. In particular, the local authority must assess the needs of disabled school leavers with statements of special educational needs for future services. The carer's ability to go on providing care must also be considered; for example if a young person is leaving school without further day provision, the carer may ask for their needs to be re-assessed.

1989 Children Act: This applies only to England and Wales; some provisions apply in Scotland. It requires local authorities to provide services for disabled children which will keep families together, including respite care. If a disabled child needs residential care, it must be suitable for their needs and near their home 'as far as is reasonably practical'. Assessment must take account of family circumstances and preferences including ethnic origin.

1990 National Health and Community Care Act: From April 1993 people already in residential care will continue to have their costs met through the DSS. Since April 1993 the local authority must assess the need of adults for respite and residential care if asked; they may provide this in their own units, but must spend at least 75% of new funds allocated on private or voluntary homes or schemes. People using residential care will be means tested to see what they can afford to pay towards the cost. There will be a limit on the amount the local authority is prepared to pay; if relatives want to use a more expensive placement, they will have to 'top-up' the fees. The situation can be complicated, so get further and up-to-date information from the organisations listed at the end of the chapter.

The written assessment must set out:

1. What the person needs

2. What the local authority will provide

You can ask for a full assessment of all care needs of the disabled person, or a partial assessment of one aspect, such as residential care.

There is a Handbook explaining what people are entitled to; this will be available at registered homes, voluntary organisations, CAB, and so on. There is a complaints procedure if you are not satisfied with any aspect of a service or are not receiving a service you think you should. You can apply to the Secretary of State for Health if you are not satisfied with the outcome of your complaint. Further information can be obtained from RADAR (address at the end of the chapter.)

There are fuller details of these laws in the *Disability Rights Handbook.*

FURTHER INFORMATION

Adoption: Parent To Parent Information Service, Lower Boddington, Daventry, Northants, NN11 6YB. Tel: 0327– 60295.

Barnardo's New Families Project, Tanners Lane, Barkingside, Ilford, Essex 1G6 1BR. Tel: 081–551–8308. To find foster parents or prospective adoptive parents for children in or going into residential care.

Blind and Physically Handicapped, Jewish Society For The, 118, Seymour Place, London W1 5DJ. Tel: 071–262–2003.

Carers National Association, 20/25 Glasshouse Yard, London EC1A 4JS. Tel: 071–490–8818. Carers Line: 171–490–8898. Information leaflets on all major aspects of the carer's role, including arranging and paying for respite and residential care; advice available on the Carers' Line.

Caresearch, Fairways, The Hudnalls, St Briavels, Lydney, Gloucestershire GL15 6SQ. Tel: 0594–530220 Computer service with details of a wide variety of care situations for people with learning disabilities.

Children's Society, Edward Rudolf House, Margery Street, London WC1X OJL. Tel: 071–837–4299. (Residential care, fostering,adoption.)

Community Service Volunteers, 237, Pentonville Road, London N1 9NJ. Tel: 071–278–6601. Independent Living Schemes.

Contact a Family, 170 Tottenham Court Road, London W1P 0HA. Tel: 071–383–3555. Factsheets; telephone helpline for parents and carers.

Crossroads Care Attendant Schemes, 10 Regent Place, Rugby, Warwicks CV21 2PN. Tel: 0788–573653. Details of local schemes offering care services within the home.

Family Based Respite Care, National Association For, Norah Fry Research Centre, University of Bristol, 32, Tyndall's Park Road, Bristol, Avon BS8 1PY. Brings together users and providers of schemes offering respite care to adults and children with severe handicaps.

Helen House Hospice for Children, All Saints Convent, 36, Leopold Street, Oxon OX4 1QT. Tel; 0865–728251. Relief care for very sick, chronically ill or dying children.

Independent Living (1993) FUND, P.O. Box 183, Nottingham, NG8 3RD. Tel: 0602–290423 or 290427.

Invalid Children's Aid Nationwide, Barbican City Gate, 1–3 Dufferin Street, London EC1Y 8NA. Tel: 071–374–4422. Advice, support, special schools, social work and welfare.

Mencap (Royal Society for Mentally Handicapped Children and Adults): 117–123 Golden Lane, London EC1Y ORT. 071–454–0454. Advice on schools, residential establishments, etc.

Parents for Children, 41 Southgate Street, London N1 3JP. Tel: 071–359–7530. Adoption and fostering agency specialising in finding homes for children with handicaps or other problems.

Radar, 12 City Forum, 250 City Road, London EC1VV 8AF. Tel: 071–250–3272. Factsheet on complaints procedures against social services departments.

Sense (Deaf/Blind and Rubella Handicaps), Head Office, 11–13, Clifton Terrace Finsbury Park London N4 3SR. Tel: 071–272–7774. Information; adult services in some regions.

Spastics Society: Callfree: Cerebral Palsy Helpline: LINKLINE 0800–626216. 12, Park Crescent, London W1N 4EQ. General telephone no. 071–636–5020.

Publications

Useful Addresses for Special Needs by Ann Worthington, MBE, 10 Norman Road, Sale, Cheshire M33 3DF. Tel: 061–905–2440. £6.75. Updated every two years. This contains many more addresses of organisations which may be helpful, and also of establishments and organisations offering respite or residential care.

Directory of Residential Accommodation for the Mentally Handicapped in England, Wales and Northern Ireland. Mencap bookshop, address above.

Disability Rights Handbook, The Disability Alliance Educational and Research Association, Universal House, 88–94, Wentworth Street, London E1 7SA. Tel: 071–247–8776. This is invaluable for all aspects of rights and provision for disability; there is a list of useful addresses towards the end. Further details of the laws mentioned in the chapter.

CHAPTER 12

INDEPENDENT LIVING ARRANGEMENTS

One of the deepest concerns of any carer is that they will become very ill or die, and the person they care for will not be looked after properly. This is one good reason for using respite care services from an early age, and considering residential options while carers are still fit and active, and can visit, and take the disabled person home to stay for periods. The adjustment to living away from home can then be made gradually, as part of the normal process of maturing and moving out of the tight family circle, instead of happening suddenly because of the severe illness or death of the carer, when the disabled person may be distressed and traumatised.

Kathy had experienced a range of residential services, some excellent for periods, some unsatisfactory and one life-threatening. When the situation deteriorated at her residential unit, we began to look at the possibility of her living in a home of her own, preferably with a similar friend, where she could be cared for with arrangements to suit her, rather than fitting into an institution. Victoria, the daughter of our close friends Jean and Norman, had a similar level of disability, and was currently in a residential unit with other young people with learning disabilities in Islington. Kathy's residential place was paid for by Islington, where we used to live. Both sets of parents wrote to Simon Palmour, Principal Officer for Learning Difficulties in Islington, and formally requested Independent Living Schemes for their daughters. Simon had worked on setting up care support packages for people with physical disabilities, and he was strongly committed to extending this practice to people with additional learning disabilities. Simon met the parents and their social workers in the summer of 1989 to discuss the basic requirements. The group agreed that we needed to:

1. identify the women's care needs

2. find suitable housing

3. obtain funding.

Regular meetings began to plan the project, and we were joined by the manager of Crossroads Care Attendant Scheme Special Projects, who was already managing extra care support to Kathy in her residential unit. They were the agency chosen to provide the care support for the project. The local Lettings Officer was also invited to meetings to ensure co-ordination of the housing services which would be needed by the two women.

The next few months were very hard work and the project would never have succeeded without the commitment and determination of all involved. Under the 1990 National Health Service and Community Care Act the idea of individually designed packages of care should become the basis of residential provision. However, local authorities have a long way to go to sort out the management implications of such schemes and, at present, where they are getting off the ground, it is due to the determination of parents, carers and voluntary groups.

I will divide the work up under the headings previously given (we were often juggling with several different aspects at the same time). It was easier to work out the various jobs that needed doing if we listed them under the headings:

1. THE CARE NEEDS

Kathy and Victoria needed twenty-four-hour care. They could not be left alone in their home for even a few minutes. Kathy was doubly incontinent and although Victoria's use of the toilet was improving, she needed to wear pads and required frequent changing. Both suffered complex and severe epileptic seizures. Both were on regular medication and Kathy's involved a long and complex list. Both suffered aches and pains arising from their disabilities and were not always able to communicate where these were. Both needed help with all aspects of personal hygiene and care. Both had exceptionally sensitive skin which required great care and attention to regular routines if it were not to break down. Both young women used wheelchairs – Kathy did not walk at all; Victoria walked for short distances only with assistance. Both could feed themselves but needed all food prepared for them. Kathy did not drink much by this stage and had fluids and medication through her naso-gastric tube; staff would need to be trained to manage this and to change the tube if necessary. Neither had any real sense of danger, so could not even be left in a room alone if they could reach and pull things down on themselves. Both communicated with their eyes, facial expressions, gestures and sounds. They shared some interests, notably a wide range of music, swimming, and going out generally. Both liked to be occupied in ways that interested them, and complained loudly if they were bored. Both enjoyed company, and were developing socially. Kathy had some day provision at a centre, but Victoria had had no formal day place since leaving school. Either could become an emergency at any time, through severe fits or some other aspect of their condition.

Through lengthy discussion of these needs and how they would be met, a pattern of staffing was drawn up which would usually provide two people on duty during waking hours, and one person to sleep in. An intercom would be installed to alert the member of staff sleeping in if one of the women was ill or distressed during the night.

2. HOUSING

The social workers helped us to apply on behalf of Kathy and Victoria to suitable housing associations, and also to the council's own wheelchair-accessible housing stock. The group agreed that they needed three-bedroomed accommodation, allowing a separate bedroom for each woman and one for the sleeping-in carer. The living room would need to be large enough to accommodate two wheelchairs; the kitchen should be large enough to eat in, and to allow Victoria and Kathy to watch food being prepared. A large bathroom would be needed for wheelchair access, with adaptations to allow access to bath, shower and toilet. An area would be needed for a washing machine and drier, and ideally a sluice should be included for dealing with soiled bedding and clothing. There should be a small garden, and parking space. There would need to be plenty of storage space for special equipment, supplies of pads and so forth.

In January 1990 they were offered one housing association property, which was nicely situated but too cramped, and relied on an internal lift for access between three floors, making washing, changing and toileting very time consuming; we were worried about relying on the lift, and it was also very small, with barely enough room for a carer to accompany the person in the wheelchair. We were disappointed, but in March were offered a purpose-built, wheelchair accessible bungalow on an council estate.

The shell was complete but the finishing work to bathroom, kitchen and utility area was left to be designed around the needs of the tenants. This involved further consultations between parents, social workers, the architect and the occupational therapist; the plans were ready by July. Islington council finally agreed to the necessary £10,000 for the extra work in December. The work was carried out in January 1991. The parents had to sign the tenancy agreement on behalf of the two women; this took some negotiation as housing found it hard to agree to allocate a tenancy to two people who could not sign an agreement and could not realistically take responsibility for meeting the terms of the tenancy in the usual way. The parents effectively had to underwrite the tenancy.

3. FUNDING

There were two aspects to this:

A. Funding for Care Costs

This was the big money! The Council had originally agreed to the project on the basis that it would not cost them any more than the current care costs for the two women. Crossroads calculated the care costs based on our discussions about the needs of the two women. To meet the shortfall, applications were made to the Independent Living Fund on behalf of both women, for funding to meet a proportion of the care costs. Both young women were visited by a representative of the Fund, and after some misunderstandings, and some delays due to their own uncertainties about government funding, a firm offer of a grant was made. Account was taken of some of their disability benefits in this allocation, meaning some of that money would also have to go towards care costs. However, we did the sums again and agreed they could manage – just. At this stage we felt we were taking an enormous risk on behalf of Kathy and Victoria – what if the funds were not sufficient, and they got into debt? The whole group shared this anxiety, so we talked it all through again and took a formal decision to go ahead.*

B. Household and Personal Expenses

Now that Kathy and Victoria were to move from residential units to their own tenancy, they would be entitled to increased benefits. However, for the first time in their lives they would also be responsible for paying all the running costs of their home – heating, lighting, water rates, telephone calls, food, cleaning materials, transport, personal expenses, garden requirements, repairs – the list seemed endless. They would also be setting up home, which

---

* The original Independent Living Fund was wound up at the end of November 1992. The funding arrangements that replace it through the Independent Living (1993) Fund are outlined in the previous chapter, Respite and Residential Care.

meant buying furniture, furnishings, household linen, utensils, household appliances, and so on. In addition, they would have to buy their own clothes and pay for any holidays or outings.*

We did the sums again and found that they would probably just manage. Applying for the changed benefits was a long saga in itself, and it took another year for Victoria's to be sorted out.

We drew up a list of essential items for setting up home – the bare minimum came to £5,000 and to provide a comfortable and appropriate environment would require nearer £10,000. The social workers applied on behalf of the two women to the Social Fund for grants towards these costs. Kathy was allocated something over £300 and Victoria twice as much; we never found out the reason for the difference. Kathy died before her appeal against this decision could be heard. The two grants just about paid for the washing machine and drier, essential items because of the double inconti-nence of both women. Friends gave second hand furniture and friends and relatives made gifts for the housewarming. MENCAP City Foundation, the North London Spastics Society and other charities made donations. We were determined that the two women would live in attractive surroundings, with good quality equipment, especially for the music which was so important to them. This all took time to achieve, but in April 1991 they were able to move into their own home, which was at least equipped with the basic require-ments for daily living.

BEFORE THEY MOVED IN

There were several tasks that had to be completed before they did move in:

1. We had to arrange for delivery and connection of appliances and furniture, clean and polish the entire bungalow, put down rugs and put up curtains, arrange things in the kitchen and the utility room.

2. We drew up instruction sheets for all the major appliances, breaking down routines into simple steps so that new staff would easily be able to operate, for example, the washing machine. We put these in plastic wallets on the walls near the appliances, and put copies in a 'House Book'.

3. We opened two building society accounts for each of the women, one to receive the ILF money and pay standing orders to the Crossroads

---

*   Disability benefits have changed since we did this, so there is no point in giving all the details. More up to date information about benefits will be found Chapter 15.

Scheme, which would provide care staff, and one for paying in benefits and drawing out money for bills, household expenses, and so forth. Jean and I spent considerable time in the local building society and had to go back more than once, but eventually staff grasped the special circumstances of two young women with profound intellectual and multiple disabilities, and we were able to open suitable accounts with arrangements for appointees to actually draw the money.

4. Arrangements with the gas, electricity and water boards took rather longer. At first they just could not cope with this situation. They wanted evidence that Jean and I had a good record for paying our own accounts. We patiently explained that the two women would be paying their bills from their benefits, and that we would guarantee this. Eventually, after many visits, telephone calls and letters, we were able to reach an agreed system.

5. The rent was covered entirely by housing benefit. The application for this was another saga, but in this case we decided not to worry about it, and when arrears notices arrived we simply referred them back to the Neighbourhood Office which was supposed to be handling both issues!

6. Both women were entitled to exemption from the Community Charge, now replaced by the Council Tax. We applied for this and there were the usual delays and muddles. We decided not to worry about this one too, and joked about possible court appearances.

7. Both women were entitled to free installation and rental of a telephone because of the severity of their disabilities; they would be responsible for payment for calls. One of the social workers applied on their behalf. The telephone duly arrived but was swiftly followed by bills for installation and rental, and threats of disconnection. We referred British Telecom to the local neighbourhood office who were handling the matter, but were more concerned about this problem, because it was quite possible the telephone would be disconnected, and this would be an unsafe situation for carers. It was sorted out eventually, but it was a worry. It was not easy to distinguish between calls made directly arising from the needs of the two women, their care and their household matters, and other calls made by care staff, such as calls to Crossroads on management matters. We agreed to operate a box system whereby staff paid what they thought the call cost, and reclaimed it from Crossroads unless it was a personal call.

8. Incontinence supplies had to be ordered from the Borough and arrangements for delivery made.

9. The occupational therapist installed an intercom system connecting the room of the carer sleeping in with the bedrooms of the two women.

10. The parents made sure that care books, information sheets and so forth, were all up to date, and available for use by workers in the bungalow. Diaries were provided and guidance given on completing them.

11. The parents set up routines for giving medication, charts for completion, systems for re-ordering supplies, including Kathy's naso-gastric tubes and syringes, and so on.

12. Crossroads arranged for care workers to work with both women in their hostels, and organised training on various aspects of their care.

13. Parents drew up a 'starter' guide to daily routines, as staff would not have the framework of a larger institution on which to rely when getting started.

14. We set up a kitty system for paying for food and other household requirements. Both sets of parents agreed to meet at the bungalow on Sunday evenings and pay in an agreed amount to be kept in a tin. We set up simple account books to note amounts paid in and for staff to note any expenditure. We set up a similar system for personal expenses for each woman.

15. New transport arrangements had to be made for Kathy to attend her day centre.

16. Kathy and Victoria had to be registered with a local GP.

It will be clear from the above points that there were many things to do, and very few of them went smoothly. There are a few examples of similar projects elsewhere, mostly still in the planning stage. Any group setting up such a project will need to plan at this level of detail.

MANAGEMENT ISSUES

The big difference between this project and other well-established independent living schemes for people with disabilities was that the two young women in this case would be unable to direct their care and would depend on other people making judgements about their best interests. When people with profound intellectual and multiple disabilities are at home, their parents do this. It involves an enormous amount of liaison with many different agencies, pulling together all the various people who meet some part of the needs of the disabled person. Whose job is it to arrange all this in an independent living scheme? And in such a scheme one can add all the extra jobs, not only managing the money but arranging for bills to be paid, repairs to be done, clothing to be bought, holidays to be arranged, and so on.

No one seems to know the answer. This scheme was planned before the new Community Care Act, but even now local authorities are only just getting to grips with their new responsibilities. Parents can do it, of course, but it should be one of the strengths of an independent living scheme that the person with the disabilities is enabled to move away gradually from the parents, and to establish their own life style. Parents will also get older, and will eventually die. Who will manage it then? Advocates have a role in representing the interests of people with disabilities, but it is not easy to get people to carry out this role, and the advocate's role is distinct from that of managing the day-to-day details of someone's life.

I have tried to show that individual care packages are possible for people with profound intellectual and multiple disabilities, but if they are to be successful two issues will need to be tackled:

1. The local authority must appoint or fund staff to manage such projects, and must work out their relationship with the agency providing the care staff, if these are not local authority employees. They may be able to oversee more than one project, but no one should underestimate the amount of time they will need to put in to replace what parents have traditionally done. Twenty hours a week would not be an exaggeration in the early stages of a project, if you count regular meetings with all concerned, and it would be difficult to do it in less than ten, even when a project is well-established. This care manager would also need to ensure regular training and up-dating of expertise for care workers.

2. There needs to be a clear operational policy for each project. This needs to be drawn up before the project starts, and all who will be concerned with the care and management of the project need to be involved, including parents. This should provide guidance on all aspects of care, management of staff, relationships between those involved in caring including family and friends, running of the household and personal relationships of the disabled people. The policy should be reviewed and revised at regular intervals. It should provide for personal care and development plans for each person with

disabilities, and these should also be reviewed and revised at regular intervals.

This kind of project can be a real step forward for many people with profound intellectual and multiple disabilities. It can be part of a natural process towards more independence from the family, while preserving the positive benefits of regular contact. It should be a real option, and should not depend on the willingness or ability of groups of parents to put in years of preparation, or to continue a level of input of many hours a week.

FURTHER INFORMATION

Independent Living (1993) Fund, P.O. Box 183, Nottingham, NG8 3RD. Tel: 0602–290423 or –290427.

For more information on the project involving Kathy and Victoria, see:

'A Home of Her Own', Pat Fitton and Jean Willson, in *Values and Visions. Changing Ideas in Services for People with Learning Difficulties.* Ed. Linda Ward and Terry Philpot. Butterworth Heinemann (1994).

Home at Last by Pat Fitton, Carol O'Brien, and Jean Willson. London: Jessica Kingsley Publishers (1995).

CHAPTER 13

WHEELCHAIRS

Once your disabled child has grown out of baby buggies, you may find you need more than one chair for different purposes. All basic wheelchairs (except occupant controlled electric wheelchairs for outdoor use) are available free of charge under the National Health Service to those who have been assessed as needing them (they are technically on loan).

Discuss the needs of the person you care for with your doctor, the hospital consultant or the physiotherapist. They will apply for you, but before they do make sure you have considered in detail the sort of wheelchair needed.

You can obtain a large size buggy, which is useful when you are travelling short distances, transferring to vehicles, buses, trains, and so on. However, the design is not supportive to anyone whose back needs firm support, and no one should sit in them for long periods. For seating, meals, longer journeys and so forth, the disabled person will need a wheelchair adapted to their specific needs. First, decide whether you want a wheelchair (two large wheels for self propelling, two smaller wheels or castors for manoeuvering) or a pushchair (four equally sized, usually 12", wheels). Can the disabled person move their own chair at all? If so, a self propelling chair would help their independence. If they do not have a strong sense of danger, you may also need a pushchair for out of doors, crossing roads, and so on. Storage begins to become a problem! You will also need to decide whether a manual or an electric wheelchair is more suitable. Is muscle weakness the main thing preventing the disabled person from pushing themselves? If so, touch controls may give them some independent movement. Is the person you care for heavy? Even if they cannot push themselves, an electric wheelchair controlled by the person behind will be less effort for the pusher, especially if they are not strong themselves, are elderly or live in a hilly area. Remember that if you have an electric wheelchair, it will be heavy and not so easy to get into a vehicle. You will also need to recharge batteries at home; the batteries are also heavy to lift out.

Often people with profound and multiple disabilities develop spinal problems, and may need special seating. There are various wedges and cushions available to make seating more comfortable. We found these insufficient for Kathy when her spinal problems increased, and she became so uncomfortable that she found it difficult to feed herself and cried to be taken out of her chair and put on the floor. She was fortunate to be referred for a matrix mould. A mould was made out of interconnecting sections, which was exactly adapted to a realistic sitting position, giving her support but allowing her to maintain some muscle control. The mould could be altered if there were postural changes. In fact she had a less restrictive mould made some years after the first, as she had become more confident in sitting and her muscle strength and control had actually improved. The other great benefit of the matrix mould is that it keeps the person in as nearly an upright position as they can manage, which is particularly important for people who are prone to chest infections. A matrix mould and other seating support systems are available under the National Health Service, but to obtain one you need a referral from a hospital consultant. Your physiotherapist will be involved in all the consultations and fitting. The mould is fixed securely to a wheelchair base and the whole thing is tested for stability. For Kathy it meant that she could feed herself again, enjoy long walks, travel long distances comfortably; it also helped to cut down on chest infections as she was so well supported. The mould comes with washable covers, made to measure.

CHECKLIST FOR CHOOSING A WHEELCHAIR

1. Talk to your GP, hospital consultant, physiotherapist.

2. Visit the Disabled Living Foundation or your local Disabled Living Centre. Details at the end of the chapter.

3. The Wolfson Centre in London will assess children for wheelchairs from all parts of the UK. They can provide overnight accommodation. Address at the end of the chapter.

4. Visit the Disablement Service Centres, which organise the distribution of wheelchairs, and ask to see the full range.

5. Read '*How to Choose a Wheelchair*' by Bert Massie and Judith Male, from RADAR, address at end of chapter.

6. If you are choosing an electric wheelchair, have you worked out the space and arrangements needed for re-charging batteries?

7. Consider whether a private wheelchair would be more suitable. There are more details about this later.

LOOKING AFTER THE WHEELCHAIR

1. When you receive a NHS wheelchair, you should get a handbook, *Hints on the use of your wheelchair*. Ask for one if it is not offered.

2. Find out how to keep the wheelchair in good condition – the base needs to be washed down regularly, especially if it gets food on it, and wheels need to be oiled sparingly. Check the brakes at least weekly, and get them adjusted immediately if they are not secure. Think about the type of belt the person using the chair needs; it should be quick release, and should always be worn whether you are out walking or travelling in a vehicle. Carry a puncture kit whenever you go out, and if possible learn to deal with the puncture yourself.

3. The Disablement Service Centre will give you details of your local approved repair company. You contact them direct for repairs. They are supposed to respond within three working days, or the same day if it is an emergency. They should operate an out-of-hours emergency service. Employees must carry an identity card. They offer a loan service if repairs cannot be carried out on site; make sure you specify what will be a suitable replacement.

4. When a wheelchair is replaced, if the old one is still safe ask to keep it as a spare.

5. Make sure that other people pushing the wheelchair know how to handle it safely. There is a useful leaflet *How to push a wheelchair* available from RADAR.

If you are not satisfied with the wheelchair provided, or do not feel you were given enough choice, first contact the person who applied for the chair. You can also contact the Disablement Service Centre direct.

If you do not feel any of the NHS models are appropriate, you can buy a private model. You might decide to use some of the mobility component of the Disability Living Allowance for this purpose. The physiotherapist or occupational therapist may be able to get it paid for through social services or some other source. The Family Fund may pay after visiting you to discuss the need. (Address at the end of the chapter.) Charities sometimes fund private wheelchairs, especially through special schools. Be sure before you spend a large sum that the chair is really suitable; get advice from the physiotherapist. Some of the private chairs look very attractive in advertisements and are marketed very strongly, but they do not always live up to expectations once you have them. Be clear what you want it to do – some things are essential, like giving good back support and being easy to clean and manoeuvre, safe and stable. You need to decide whether you will be mainly using it outdoors or inside, or whether you want something suitable for both, whether you will need to transport it in a vehicle and in that case whether it folds or can be dismantled into separate pieces.

CHECKLIST FOR CHOOSING A PRIVATE WHEELCHAIR

1. Read *How to Choose a Wheelchair* referred to earlier.

2. Check whether the company advertising the product belongs to either the British Association of Wheelchair Distributors or the British Surgical Trades Association – addresses at the end of the chapter; they have strict codes of practice.

3. Ask to try several models at home.

4. Various models are on view at the Disabled Living Foundation or your local Disabled Living Centre.

5. There is a VAT zero rating for use by a disabled person.

6. Ask what after-sales-service is provided.

7. Arrange insurance; this is not necessary for NHS wheelchairs but essential for a wheelchair you have purchased or which has been bought on your behalf, for example. by a charity.

FURTHER INFORMATION

Publications

How to Choose a Wheelchair by Bert Massie and Judith Male. Available from RADAR, address below.

How to push a wheelchair by Bert Massie and Judith Male. Available from RADAR, address below.

Addresses

British Association of Wheelchair Distributors, 1 Webbs Court, Buckhurst Avenue, Sevenoaks, Kent TN13 1LZ. Tel: 0732–458868.

British Surgical Trades Association, 1 Webbs Court, Buckhurst Avenue, Sevenoaks, Kent TN13 1LZ. Tel: 0732–458868.

Disabled Living Foundation, 380–384 Harrow Road, London W9 2HU. Tel: 071–289–6111. Advice, information and demonstration of equipment. They produce detailed and practical leaflets on many aspects of equipment for disability. You need to make an appointment to visit.

Family Fund, PO Box 50, York, YO1 2ZX. Tel: 0904–621115. They help with the cost of equipment needed by families caring for a severely handicapped child. Contact them to discuss your needs. They also produce a booklet on benefits and services for people over 16 with severe disabilities.

RADAR, Royal Association for Disability and Rehabilitation, 12 City Forum, 250 City Road, London EC1V 8AF. Tel: 071–250–3222. Advice and publications.

The Wolfson Centre, Mecklenburgh Square, London WC1N 2AP. Tel: 071–837–7618.

CHAPTER 14

MOBILITY, EQUIPMENT AND ADAPTATIONS

When you are caring for a baby with profound and multiple disabilities, much of the usual equipment will do, except for some specialised needs. As the baby grows older and bigger, she will still need many of the care, seating and mobility aids but in larger sizes and adapted more to her individual needs. I will discuss these needs under separate headings:

1. VEHICLES AND MOTORING

Comfort and safety for the person with profound intellectual and multiple disabilities must be your first consideration. Travelling can be a real pleasure for someone who cannot move independently, but they cannot enjoy it if they are not comfortable. If you are driving, your decision about the type of vehicle to use will depend on whether the disabled person is going to travel in their wheelchair or transfer into a car seat or harness. You can get specialist car seats and harnesses for babies and young children with disabilities. Once they have grown larger, they will often be more comfortable in their own wheelchair. Now you may need a specially adapted car or even a van. There are various ways of travelling with a wheelchair in use – the following give you some idea:

1. A car or van with a raised roof to take the wheelchair in the back, and a ramp or car floor that lowers to take the wheelchair on.
2. A larger van with a tail lift fitted to take the wheelchair on board.
3. A larger van with a ramp to take the wheelchair on board.

Remember that, if you are handling an electric wheelchair, it will be heavy and therefore more difficult to get into a vehicle. A lift may be essential rather than a ramp.

In all cases, you must have secure arrangements for fastening the wheelchair to the vehicle floor. There are various methods available, most some variation on straps or bolts. In all cases the fixings must go through the vehicle floor to ensure security. The person must also be fastened securely in their wheelchair, and if the chair can be separated into different parts, these must be secured.

Our own solution, for cheapness and convenience, was to use a Sherpa van. A garage fitted a ramp to the side door, and we wheeled Kathy in her chair up into place, and then fastened the chair with straps which were fixed through the van floor. She was comfortable and, because of her high position, had a good view while we were travelling. The large van gave us room to install a platform for changing her pads and generally seeing to her, and we put curtains up so these could be drawn to give privacy when doing this. In the period before she died we were reconsidering the arrangements and had decided to put a seat in the back next to her, as her fits were more frequent and she needed more close supervision. The platform was also useful when she did have a severe fit, as we could give her rectal valium and keep her in the recovery position afterwards.

You can get full information on choosing a vehicle from the Department of Transport, Mobility Information Service and the Banstead Mobility Centre (addresses at end of chapter).

A vehicle used by or for some disabled people can get exemption from Road Tax (Vehicle Excise Duty). There were some changes to the scheme for those applying after 13th October 1993. If the person you care for is getting the higher rate mobility part of Disability Living Allowance (see the next chapter) you can apply on their behalf for a certificate of entitlement to the Disability Living Allowance unit. (The address is at the end of the next chapter.) When you receive the certificate, take or send it to your nearest Vehicle Registration Office with your vehicle registration documents, insurance certificate and test certificate if needed. You can fill in a vehicle licence application form V10 there, or get one at the post office and send it. They will then give you a tax exempt disc. Two important things to remember:

1. The vehicle must be registered in the name of the disabled person or, in certain cases, their nomineee.

2. The exemption will only apply if the vehicle is being used 'solely by or for the purposes of the disabled person'. This could mean travelling in

it, picking up or dropping off, or collecting items like prescriptions or shopping specifically for them.

You will need to apply for an Orange Badge to obtain parking concessions; this will be handled by your local social services office. There will usually be no problem in obtaining it on behalf of someone with profound intellectual and multiple disabilities. Orange Badges are issued at the discretion of local authorities; some ask you to get a doctor's letter to confirm the need. If you are refused, there is no formal right of appeal and you would need to contact your local advice centre or a local councillor. The Orange Badge should not be used unless the disabled person is travelling on that journey, or being picked up or dropped off.

Motability will help people with disabilities who are receiving the higher rate mobility part of the Disability Living Allowance to buy or lease a specially adapted vehicle. (The address is at the end of the chapter.)

If you do not drive, you will want to use transport services developed for people with disabilities. These fall into three main categories:

1. Mobility buses – these have low platforms and access for wheelchairs. They are not available in all areas and arrangements vary according to the locality. In London there is an adapted bus service, Careline, linking the main rail stations.

2. Adapted taxis – sometimes called black cabs; the new metro cabs have doors opening to a right angle, a portable ramp and wheelchair fixings. You may be able to obtain cheap fares through a taxi card system.

3. Dial-a-ride systems. Exact details vary according to area, but generally these offer minibuses adapted to take wheelchairs. The disabled person joins the scheme, and you are told how to make bookings.

British Rail offer some concessions for a disabled traveller and a companion. There are facilities for taking wheelchairs into some carriages, and varying amounts of assistance at stations. The situation has not improved a great deal in the last ten years, and you may still find yourself travelling with someone in a wheelchair in the guard's van. It remains to be seen whether privatisation will improve the situation. (Contact details for information at the end of the chapter.)

Transport to hospital can be a problem. If you are taking someone with profound intellectual and multiple disabilities, you are entitled to transport. However, you may find that you are waiting around for long periods before being collected, or collected very early and then waiting for hours at the hospital. You may then face a further wait after the appointment. Sometimes the transport is cancelled, or arrives so late that you miss the appointment. Ambulances are not necessarily able to transport someone in their electric wheelchair. Using your own transport can be difficult, as parking is not always easy at hospitals. We found it was best to use a taxi in London, but this would be expensive for a very long journey. If you have to travel to hospital very frequently, for treatment or consultation, you should contact your local social services or the social worker at the hospital to see what help can be arranged with transport.

2. ADAPTATIONS TO THE HOME

Grants are available for work to be carried out which will give the person with disabilities:

1. better access to and from the home

2. easier use of the main family room

3. better access to, use of and if necessary provision of a bedroom.

4. better access to, use of and if necessary provision of facilities for washing and toileting.

5. improving or providing any heating system to meet the needs of the disabled person.

There are other provisions, but I have listed the ones most likely to apply to someone with profound intellectual and multiple disabilities.

You apply to the local authority, and the social services department will arrange a visit to assess the need. The local authority has to agree to works if they are necessary for the carer to continue caring, and for the disabled person to remain within the home. Any work must be done for the benefit of the disabled person and they must usually live in the home. It is possible to get agreement for work if you regularly have a disabled person home, even when they live some of the time elsewhere. Grants are means tested. If the disabled person is not the owner or tenant, the income of the owner or tenant will be taken into account as well when assessing the amount of grant. You can get more information from '*The Disability Rights Handbook*' (address at the end of the chapter).

You will want to consider carefully what sort of adaptations will make life easier. Ramps to the entrances, wider doors, knocking two rooms into one, installing a lift or stair lift, even building an extension – you may find you need one or more of these or other solutions. You may need further work done as the disabled person grows older or gets bigger, or perhaps develops further special requirements. You may want to get further information from the Disabled Living Foundation. You can find out the address of your nearest Disabled Living Centre from the Disabled Living Centres Council (addresses at the end of the chapter).

Think through the effect of adaptations on the general running of the home and others in the family. When we moved with Kathy into a three-storey Victorian house, we were offered a grant for a purpose-built extension for all her care needs. We decided instead that we wanted to keep her within the main rooms of the house, and we opted instead for relatively minor alterations such as double-hinged doors that you could back into with the wheelchair. As Kathy remained physically small we preferred to carry her up to bed so she was near our room at night, and her bedroom was chosen because it was next to the bathroom. She was carried downstairs in the morning and her care needs for the rest of the day were met there. We had a large bed sofa specially made for changing her, for laying her down during fits and giving rectal valium, and where she could rest or sleep if she was unwell, while still being with the rest of the family. We did have a sluice installed in place of the downstairs toilet. Kathy did not use the toilet and the sluice was an enormous help in dealing with soiled clothes and bedding, saving much slopping about with buckets. If you did not have space or could not afford to give up a toilet, it would be still be worth exploring ways of having a sluice installed.

Your main problem will be the shortage of occupational therapists, who usually do these assessments; this leads to long waiting times after you have applied.

There may be other considerations if you are caring for someone who has sensory disabilities. If they have impaired sight it is worth considering the colours you use when re-decorating your home. A contrasting colour on a door surround, for instance, will make it easier to enter or leave a room, and even if the disabled person is not very mobile, they will make more sense of rooms and of other people coming in and out. Similarly, you might look at the colour and type of carpet you choose. Lighting will be very important – you need to consider the brightness and position of lights, and which type of bulb you use.

If someone has a hearing impairment you can help them to enjoy music and television by using loop systems. You can get a doorbell which flashes a light when it rings, or one with a fan which can be felt by someone who is deaf-blind. Even if they are not able to answer the door, they will be aware of people's comings and goings, and both feel involved in and make more sense of what is going on.

You can get specialist advice on these and other ideas from SENSE, RNIB and RNID. (Details at the end of this chapter; you will also find details of magazines which give information and ideas for people with sensory disabilities).

You will not get grants for your garden, but if you have one, it is worth considering it as another room or facility for the person with disabilities. You may change the layout so that it is convenient and pleasant for them to sit or lie outside; you can choose plants which are scented, or have interesting textures and shapes. You may want to consider how the person with disabilities can join others to eat outside. There are good ideas in the PRMH Leisure pack (details at the end of the 'Leisure' chapter). Kathy liked to lie outside on a rug and cushions, playing with favourite objects, and looking at the light and shadows. We laid meadow grass, which gave her a thick cushion, and included flowers which bloomed at different times for her to watch and touch; we put shrubs and small trees where they could give dappled shade, protecting her from the sun and giving her additional pleasure in watching the patterns. She enjoyed eating outside, so we made sure her wheelchair could join a group round the garden table. Even if your garden or yard is small, careful thought and planning can make it a restful and pleasant place, for the person with disabilities as well as everyone else.

If you are a local council, housing association or private tenant, you may apply to the council for transfer to accommodation which has been built or adapted for easy access for someone using a wheelchair. Local authorities must consider the needs of disabled people in any new housing schemes. Ask your social worker, or contact the local social services office first.

3. EQUIPMENT FOR DAILY LIVING

Local authorities must provide equipment needed to help people with disabilities live in their homes. You may need a hoist or other help for the disabled person to get in and out of the bath, shower or bed; special seats or supports for using the toilet; an intercom or alarm system when you are in a different part of the house from the person with the disabilities; specially adapted furniture; equipment for feeding, and so forth. Community health services have similar responsibilities for 'nursing equipment' which might include special beds, commodes, and so on.

Apply to your doctor for any of these needs first. If you see any of the following regularly, you can apply through them – community nurse, health visitor, occupational therapist or physiotherapist.

If you do not have a telephone, this must be provided if it is necessary for the person with disabilities to be safely cared for. Apply to your local social services. They pay for installation and rental; you pay for calls.

The right feeding equipment can help many people with multiple disabilities to develop some independence in eating and drinking. Ask the occupational therapist what they can supply, but equipment does not have to be highly specialised. You can build up cutlery yourself with foam, making it easier to grip. If you can find the right shape of bowl with a lip to stop food sliding off the edge you will not need a plateguard. You can get non-slip mats to put under bowls; a plastic soap gripper will also do. Large branches of some retail chemists have dishes, cups and cutlery which may be suitable.

Clothing can be a problem. I found Kathy was more comfortable in the wheelchair and on the floor in loose trousers; she wore dresses and tights for special occasions. There are specialist clothing suppliers – your local Disabled Living Centre will have details. Most parents and carers find by experience what suits the person they care for. Clothing generally needs to be loose, no tight necks, cuffs or armholes, and in natural fibres where possible to avoid skin irritation. Tops are easier to take on and off if they open at least part of the way. If someone is out in a wheelchair on a hot day they need a sun hat. They also get cold more quickly when temperatures are low, so a hat, gloves, warm socks and a scarf are essential, as well as a padded jacket. Everything should be washable. It is so important for someone with profound intellectual and multiple disabilities to feel and look good in their clothes, and they should be involved in choosing them as much as possible. We took Kathy to the shops and she found ways of letting us know which colours and styles she preferred; if we were ordering by post we would look through the catalogues with her.

If you protect clothing during meals you cut down on washing. You can get PVC aprons in all sizes; if you need to protect cuffs, you can get plastic painting aprons and cuffs from some toy shops. I always put something absorbent on top of the pvc apron, or I found food and drink often slithered off the bottom onto trousers and the floor. You can make large bibs from towelling. We bought some very attractive bibs for Kathy which were the largest I have seen, and did not look ridiculous even on an adult. The brand name was de Witte Lietaer, and we got a department store to order some for us when they were not in stock.

Not everyone agrees with using bibs for adults who dribble. I found Kathy's clothes got very damp, she was uncomfortable and her mouth and chin got sore, unless she wore bibs. I regarded them as part of her clothing and she and I chose them very carefully.

I have mentioned shoes and boots later under 'Appliances'. If the person you care for needs specialised footwear, including slippers, you can get these through the NHS or from specialised companies; the Disabled Living Foundation has details.

Toys are an essential part of daily living for children. Many everyday objects are just as much fun as expensive toys for all children – egg whisks, plastic cups and plates, clothes pegs, washing up bowls. Kathy loved all kinds of brushes. Empty and clean plastic bottles and containers filled with rice, beans and buttons make good shakers. You can make simple activity boards with different materials for texture, bells and other objects to make sounds and items with different smells. You can sew cloth bags or cover cardboard boxes with attractive paper, and fill them with objects of interest. Kathy had bags and boxes with different types of things, for example, bells and shakers. When she got tired of one set, she could be offered a choice of others.

I have given details at the end of the chapter of a book (*Space and Self*) which makes many practical suggestions for toys and play activities especially for blind children and those with multiple disabilities. I have also included the Play Matters (Toy Libraries Association) address; they have information about toys suitable for children with disabilities and addresses of local toy libraries.

Adults will have favourite objects and activities, and some may still be interested in things they used when they were younger. They should not be deprived of these because of notions that they are no longer appropriate. You want to go on developing new interests and activities for the person you care for, but in the end it is their right to choose things and activities which give them pleasure and enjoyment, just as we would.

4. INCONTINENCE EQUIPMENT AND SUPPLIES

I have put this under a separate heading because managing incontinence with dignity is such hard work. Most people with profound intellectual and multiple disabilities will have some degree of incontinence, and you may be caring for someone with double incontinence.

Health authorities have powers to give the following help in the way of equipment and supplies, free of charge:

- loan of a commode and bed linen;

- protective pants;
- interliners;
- pads or nappies;
- disposable drawsheets;
- protective sheets and pillow cases;
- bed pans and bottles.

Local authorities can provide the following free services:

1. A laundry service – soiled sheets, bedding, clothes and nappies can be collected and returned laundered.

2. A waste disposal services for soiled incontinence pads, dressings, etc.

Problems

1. The type and amount of help, and how you get it, varies from area to area. Ask your doctor if there is a Continence Adviser for a start; if so, they can sort out what you need and which services are provided by health and which by social services. If there is no such person, ask to speak to the Information Officer of the local council. If you still cannot get adequate information, get in touch with your local Community Health Council, who can find out for you.

2. You may only be supplied with the type of pads, and other equipment that the authority normally gives out. These may not be suitable for the person you care for. We found the larger version of the all-in-one pads used by babies and toddlers more convenient than separate pads and pants. You may also be told there is a restriction on the amount of supplies. We had to fight quite hard to get the right pads for Kathy and the right amounts as, in addition to being doubly incontinent, she suffered from a bowel disorder which caused constant and copious diarrhoea. If you run into difficulties, ask your doctor or consultant for a letter outlining the medical reasons for your request; if it is a regular order there should be no problem with health or social services ordering something slightly different. Contact your Community Health Council if you still have problems. There is a display of equipment for managing incontinence at the Disabled Living Foundation.

3. You may find the laundry services is infrequent and you are having to store soiled linen. You may also need to buy extra quantities of everything to allow for the waiting period for the return of clean laundry.

4. You may find delivery of supplies is only possible at a time decided by the authorities. We had supplies dumped on the doorstep as 'the driver could not wait for an answer'. Had they been stolen we would not have known; or it might have rained!

You can buy incontinence requirements from some chemists or specialist suppliers, but it is expensive to do this for any length of time. You may decide to do this for a short period, or for a special time such as a holiday, but do insist on getting what the disabled person really needs from the local authorities. You can contact RADAR (address at end of chapter) if you think you are not getting services you are legally entitled to.

Protection for bedding – and for furniture such as settees – is important and saves work and expense in the long run. Plastic covers can be hot and sweaty. We found some excellent protection which was a coated nylon – you can get fitted bed sheets, pillow cases, duvet covers and draw sheets; the firm will make items to measure. (The address is at the end of the chapter.) We put protective covers under loose covers on some of our furniture, so that Kathy could sit with us for a cuddle; then at the worst we had to wash the covers.

An automatic washing machine and tumble drier takes the aggravation out of constant washing. If you find it difficult to afford or replace such equipment, and you have a disabled child aged sixteen or under, you can apply to the Family Fund for help. (Address at the end of the chapter.) If you are receiving benefits as income, you may be entitled to a grant for purchase of a machine, which may be re-conditioned. Local charities or voluntary groups for a particular disability may also be able to help.

5. APPLIANCES ETC.

I am including here items needed to maintain the condition of the disabled person or to prevent things getting worse, such as splints and braces. I would also include special footwear, hearing aids, low vision aids, and so forth. If you are attending hospital regularly with a disabled child, you will usually ask the doctor for any such needs, or she may suggest them. The doctor may then refer you to a physiotherapist or appliance officer to sort out what is needed. If you have a child at special school some items may be arranged through visiting specialists. Items such as splints and braces may need renewing frequently, either through wear and tear or because they are outgrown, or the condition changes. Kathy wore wrist splints to try and prevent the rheumatoid arthritis causing the joints to drop. The day splints allowed her to use her hands for most activities, although we took them off for feeding; the night splints kept her fingers as straight as possible, restricting her movement. She chewed both sets so they needed renewing fairly frequently, and she was ingenious at finding ways of removing them, so we and the physiotherapists had to be quite inventive about fastenings. All splints and braces can be an ordeal to have fitted, as it means staying still for long periods. It is worth persevering as they can prevent some deformities from getting worse; a back brace can sometimes avoid the need for an operation if it is worn correctly and regularly. In hot weather they get very sweaty; take them off for a rest, or use thin cotton tubing to protect the skin.

If special footwear is needed, ask what the possibilities are. Hospitals often supply particular ranges because they have dealt with certain companies for a long time. You need to make sure the footwear is suitable for the disabled person, and it also needs to be as attractive as possible. You can get slippers as well, with easy fastenings for difficult feet. For a long time Kathy was regularly prescribed quite sturdy leather ankle boots, even though she would never walk. We eventually found details of some light felt boots which still gave good support, but were less heavy for her thin legs and looked good, and the hospital agreed to supply these instead.

6. MEDICAL EQUIPMENT

The disability itself or other medical problems may mean using particular items in the daily routine, such as catheters, naso-gastric tubes, syringes, and so on. These are not available on prescription in the usual way from your GP. Hospitals and health authorities vary in their systems for issuing these. You need to talk to the consultant in the first place, and work out a reliable system to obtain what you need. We found no problem in obtaining such supplies while Kathy was attending the children's hospital, but as soon as she transferred to the adult hospital we ran into problems, even though the consultant had authorised issue of supplies. Eventually the administrator responsible put us in touch with the person in charge of the stores. He worked out a very simple system – he put Kathy's name on a shelf and ordered supplies of the items she needed. Whenever we collected items, he would replace so that there was always a supply in stock. If you cannot collect items, then the health authority must make arrangements to deliver them.

REGISTERING AS DISABLED

The person you care for can be registered as disabled at any age with the local authority; the disability has to be 'substantial and permanent'. If you have a social worker, they can visit you to go through the registration form. If not, ask your local social services office to arrange for someone to visit you and do this. You will receive a card or letter confirming the registration.

You can get services without being registered, but it is better for the local authority to have accurate details of the numbers and needs of disabled people in their area for better planning of services. It also means the disabled person is 'on the books', and this may act as a short-cut in dealing with some matters.

THE LAW

It is useful to know what must be done and provided, so that you can insist if you are refused something. Apart from medical requirements, many of the above items or works must be provided under the 1970 Chronically Sick and Disabled Persons Act, once the local authority has agreed to the need; this was extended to Scotland in 1972 and Northern Ireland in 1978. The 1981 Disabled Persons Act made further provision, especially on improving access. The 1986 Disabled Persons (Services, Consultation and Representation) Act made some of the best good practice a legal requirement.

Under the 1986 Act a disabled person and their carer have the right to ask the local authority social services to assess their need for any of the welfare services listed in the Act.

If you care for a disabled child, she will be entitled to assessment for provision and services under the 1989 Children Act.

Social services must tell disabled people and their carers of the range of services available to them under these laws.

If you are refused any item or service, first ask your social worker to take it up; or contact the Director of Social Services; or your local councillor. If you still have difficulty, contact RADAR for advice. If you are making contact with social services for the first time, you will find them in the telephone book under the name of the local authority where you live, for example, Brent Borough Council; then look under that list for social services, then for the office nearest to where you live.

FURTHER INFORMATION:

Publications

How to get Equipment for Disability, Michael Mandelstam. ISBN 185302 190 3.
3rd edition 1993. Published by Jessica Kingsley and Kogan Page for the
Disabled Living Foundation. This large handbook is most likely to be used
by professionals and organisations responsible for prescribing and supplying
equipment for people with disabilities. It is divided into sections dealing
with an aspect of need, such as Mobility, Equipment for people with
hearing impairment, and so on. It gives considerable detail about available
aids and equipment, the criteria for agreeing to their supply and the relevant
laws. Complaints procedures are outlined and there are examples of how
some complaints were dealt with. A parent or carer may find this book
useful when investigating a particular aspect of supply of equipment, to find
out all the possibilities, and for help in dealing with any problems in
obtaining what is needed. Ask for it in the reference library, or ask one of
the professionals you deal with such as a physiotherapist if you can consult
a copy.

The Disability Rights Handbook, updated every year. From: The Disability
Alliance Educational and Research Association, Universal House, 88–94
Wentworth Street, London E1 7SA. Tel; 071–247–8776. This gives
checklists of what you are entitled to, advice about applying, and details of
where you may get even more detailed advice.

Space and Self by Lilli Nielsen. SIKON (1992). ISBN 87 503 9566 1. Ideas for
toys and play with blind children and those with multiple disabilities.

*Toy Workshop: Toys You Can Make Yourself for Handicapped and Non-Handicapped
Children*. ISBN 3 924830 3 4. Available from Jessica Kingsley Publishers.

Addresses

British Rail, Dept. XX. PO Box 28, York YO1 1FB. Tel: 0904–653022.
Information about the railcard for disabled people and general facilities; or
ask at your nearest main line station.

Disabled Living Centres Council. 76 Clarendon Park Road, Leicester
LE2 3AD. Tel: 0533–793140. They have details of local Disabled Living
Centres.

Disabled Living Foundation, 380–384 Harrow Road, London W9 2HU. Tel:
071–289–6111. Advice, information and demonstration of equipment.
They produce detailed and practical leaflets on many aspects of equipment
for disability. You need to make an appointment to visit.

Driver Vehicle and Licensing Centre, Vehicle Enquiry Unit Centre, Longview Road, Swansea SA6 7JL. Contact them if you want information about exemption from road tax (vehicle excise duty).

Family Fund, PO Box 50, York, YO1 2ZX. Tel: 0904–621115. They help with the cost of equipment needed by families caring for a severely handicapped child. Contact them to discuss your needs. They also produce a booklet on benefits and services for people over 16 with severe disabilities.

Mobility Centre, Banstead. Damson Way, Orchard Hill, Queen Mary's Avenue, Carshalton, Surrey. Tel: 081–770–1151. Advice and information on different types of vehicles suitable for disabled people.

Mobility Information Service, Unit 2a, Atcham Industrial Estate, Upton Magna, Shrewsbury SY4 4UG. Tel: 0743–761889. Information on vehicles, adaptations, costs, for buying or adapting vehicles for disabled people.

Motability, Gate House, Westgate, The High, Harlow, Essex CM20 1HR. Tel: 0279–635666. Details of buying or hiring vehicles for disabled people.

Network for the Handicapped, 16 Princeton Street, London WC1R 4BB. Tel: 071–831–8031/7740. Legal advice on rights of people with disabilities.

Play Matters (Toy Libraries Association), 68 Church Way, London NW1 1LT. Tel: 071–387–9592.

RADAR, Royal Association for Disability and Rehabilitation, 12 City Forum, 250 City Road, London EC1V 8AF. Tel: 071–250–3222. Advice and publications, including leaflet on Complaints Procedure about social services provision.

RNIB Resource Centre, 224 Great Portland Street, London W1N 6AA. Tel: 071–388–1266. Information on equipment, aids etc. for blind or partially-sighted people.

RNID National Technology and Information Centre, 4 Church Road, Edgbaston, Birmingham B15 3TD. Parent's Freephone: 0800–424545.

SENSE (National Deaf-Blind Rubella Association), Head Office, 11–13, Clifton Terrace, Finsbury Park, London N4 3SR. Tel: 071–272–7774. SENSE have regional centres; head office will tell you about the one nearest to you. They offer parent groups, advice and information.

Squires Protective Bedding, Unit 35, Staveley Workshops, Works Road, Hollingwood, Chesterfield, Derbys. S43 2EE. Tel: 0246–475225. Suppliers of protective covers, made of various grades of nylon material. Will make to measure.

Transport, Department of, Mobility Unit, Room S10/20, 2 Marsham Street, London SW1P 3EB. Tel: 071–276–4973. Offer advice and information for disabled people about mobility and transport.Publish 'Door to Door' a guide to transport for people with disabilities. Free to voluntary organisations etc; can be bought from HMSO.

Whitefields Special Needs Library, Macdonald Road, Walthamstow, London E17 4AZ. Tel: 071–531–3426.

Magazines

Information Exchange. Ideas on all aspects of life with someone with multiple disabilities. Very practical. Contact Ken Wood, 53 The Circuit, Cheadle Hulme, Cheadle, Cheshire SK8 7LF. Tel: 061–486–6514.

Eye Contact, Focus and *Visability:* information and practical ideas for those with a visual disability. Details from RNIB, address above.

CHAPTER 15

BENEFITS

This chapter concentrates on benefits likely to apply to people with profound intellectual and multiple disabilities. It briefly outlines what is available, but mainly gives guidance on applying and on dealing with delays or refusals. Whole books are written and updated annually on benefits, and many organisations such as MENCAP have an officer who specialises in benefit regulations; there are also local advice centres, Citizens Advice Bureaux, law centres, and so forth, which can help. (Details are given at the end of this chapter.) There are various leaflets on benefits which you can pick up at the post office, the local library, some GPs' surgeries or the local Social Security office. MENCAP have a list of the leaflets for different benefits. Details of the Benefits Agency helplines are given at the end.

Where do you start? So many parents hear by chance of benefits which are available for their child, years after they began to be entitled to them. Social workers and other general advice workers do not always know of the specialised aspects of benefits for disabled people. Contact a Family and Carers National Association produce factsheets summarising benefits available to disabled people; RADAR include a summary of benefits as well as other basic rights and services in their useful booklet for newly disabled people, *If Only I'd Known that a Year Ago*.

The names of benefits and the arrangements for applying for them change frequently. The rules sometimes change about who is entitled to some benefits. It is essential to get up to date information from the organisations and publications listed in the reference section at the end of the chapter. The following notes concentrate on how to organise your applications, what to do if things do not go smoothly and where to get further information. The notes are arranged according to the type of benefit, using the current names.

1. BENEFITS FOR SOMEONE NEEDING EXTRA CARE

Disability Living Allowance is in two parts:

(i) 'Care component' awarded at higher, middle or lower rates according to the amount of care needed (formerly Attendance Allowance.)

(ii) 'Mobility component' awarded at higher or lower rates, depending on how difficult it is for the person to walk or get about independently (formerly Mobility Allowance.)

It is tax free, not means tested and the disabled person need not have made national insurance contributions.

If the person claiming is over 65 they claim Attendance Allowance for care needs, and the mobility component of DLA if they have difficulty in getting about. If the person claiming has a terminal illness, the Attendance Allowance or DLA care component is processed quickly under special rules.

You apply by sending for the claim pack; phone the Benefits Agency Helpline 0800–88 22 00, complete the post-paid coupon in the leaflet on DLA, or call in to your local Benefits Agency office. If payments are agreed, they start from the day you requested your claim pack, so do this as quickly as possible.

You will get two forms to complete, and it looks like an enormous task. First, show the forms to your social worker if you have one, and any friends who have claimed for a disabled member of the family; you might want to talk to an advice service too. You will be asked for a great deal of detailed information about the needs of the disabled person, and your answers will be used to decide on the level of benefit, or whether to give any at all. There are full details of the requirements in the *Disability Rights Handbook*. In deciding claims, the Benefits Agency use the *Disability Handbook*, which is a guide to how much care and help with mobility different disabilities and conditions are likely to give rise to. You can buy a copy of this (the MENCAP bookshop have it or you can ask for it to be ordered by a local bookshop) or consult it in your local library. You may find it useful to look through this and see what it says the care needs are for the particular conditions of the person you care for.

Photocopy the forms and begin to fill the copies in roughly. Take it step by step; if you work your way steadily through the forms, they do give you help in answering the questions as they come up. Take every opportunity to give full details of what has to be done. When you have completed in rough all but the last two sections, you can copy everything neatly on the original forms. If you find it difficult to complete any of the sections, or the whole

thing, you can get help over the telephone to complete it: ask the Helpline.
A Home Visitor to help with this may be possible; ask if they can organise
this if you would prefer it. If you do this, make sure you have rough notes
or someone to help you, so that everything you need to say is actually written
down. The last two sections are for brief statements about the disabilities or
conditions and how they affect the person you are claiming for. The first
one can be filled in by the main carer. The second one needs to be filled in
by the GP, hospital consultant, physiotherapist or someone similar who
knows the person and their disabilities. Make sure you do these things:

(i)   Complete the form with a black pen.

(ii) Keep your completed photocopied forms. (They get lost sometimes –
      you do not want to have to do all this again.)

(iii) Check that both forms are signed where required, especially the last
      section mentioned above.

(iv) Return the form by the second date stamped on the front page, or you
      may lose benefit.

(v)   If you have not had an acknowledgement within two weeks, phone
      the Helpline or write and ask for one.

(vi) If there are further delays do not hesitate to contact your local advice
      centre, social worker, etc. The MENCAP Benefits Officer will give
      you details of local advice services.

(vii) Keep everything to do with this matter in one place – use a plastic or
      cardboard wallet or a large envelope to keep papers together. Write
      down on the front any reference numbers you are given so you have
      them handy. Keep copies of all forms you complete and all letters you
      write, however short. Put dates on any letters you write.

When making enquiries about your claim, to the Helpline or by letter:

(i)   Name the benefit you are claiming.

(ii) Give the surname of the person you are claiming for.

(iii) Give the national insurance number if the disabled person has one.

(iv) Phone the Helpline or the Benefits Centre (the address will be on
      correspondence and forms) **not** the local Benefits Agency office, as
      they will not be so well informed.

(v)   You can ask 'Who am I speaking to?' and they will give you a name;
      you should make a note of this in case there is a problem later. You
      can then say, 'But on 6th June Sean MacDonald told me…'

If the Benefits Agency want more information, they may ask for further medical evidence or send a DSS doctor to visit. Discuss this with your GP or hospital consultant; have your partner, a friend or your social worker with you for the DSS doctor's visit. Remember, they will not know the disabled person, and you will have to give very full information about their care and mobility needs.

What if your claim is refused?

(i)   You can ask for a review within three months.

(ii) You can appeal within three months if that review decision goes against your claim:

    (a) On a point of law – to a Social Security Appeal Tribunal.

    (b) On medical grounds – to a Disability Appeal Tribunal.

(iii) If you lose again on (a) you can apply for leave to appeal to the Social Security Commissioners. If you lose on (b) you can ask for another review.

(iv) You can ask for further reviews if the condition of the disabled person deteriorates.

(v)   You can ask for a further review if the disabled person becomes very seriously ill – ask for a review under Special Rules.

You should get advice at all stages of reviews and appeals. It may be that you are not giving full information, or in a way they accept. The disabled person you care for may have a very complex condition, and they may not have come across this before. You need legal advice if you appeal on a point of law.

Check if DLA is awarded with a time limit; this may be the case with children. You will need to re-apply in good time before the time limit is up.

Babies may be awarded DLA care component from birth if they are terminally ill. Other babies can get it if they need special care over and above that normally given to infants their age; for example, if they are being fed by tube. Children can be awarded DLA if their care needs are considerably more than those of other children of their age.

2. BENEFITS FOR THE CARER

You can claim Invalid Care Allowance (ICA) if you spend at least 35 hours a week caring for a severely disabled person. You do not have to live with the disabled person. You can claim for part of the year, for example. in school holidays. If you get ICA, the person you care for cannot claim Severe

Disability Premium (see below.) ICA is not means tested and you do not have to have paid national insurance contributions; but it is taxable. You need to check on the age limits for claiming, and the current limits on what you can earn part time. If you get other benefits they may be reduced by the amount of ICA; if you get some benefits you cannot receive ICA because they 'overlap'. However, it is still worth claiming, first, because it entitles you to a carer premium which is taken into account when Income Support and other benefits are assessed, so you may receive more benefit in total; and second, because there are other advantages which may improve future entitlement to benefits, which may apply to you. See the *Disability Rights Handbook* for full details.

Get the leaflet on ICA from the post office; you can get an application form there, or from your local Benefits Agency office. Ring the Benefit Enquiry Line for further information or advice. Details at the end of the chapter. Keep copies of all application forms and any correspondence.

3. BENEFITS TO GIVE INCOME

(i)   If you are getting Income Support, you can claim disabled child premium for a child who is registered as blind, gets DLA, or would get it if they were not in hospital. The premium will not be paid if the child has savings over current limits. Check with your advice centre.

(ii) Severe Disablement Allowance (SDA) can be claimed by a young person coming up to age 16 who is unlikely to be able to work because of illness or disability. She can draw this allowance even while she is at school, but it might depend on whether all or part of her education is specifically for people with a mental or physical disability. This benefit is not means tested, not taxable and does not require national insurance contributions. It is less than Income Support but should be claimed for someone with profound intellectual and multiple disabilities. You can then claim Income Support as a top up. You can get the leaflet on SDA at the post office. This will tell you how to apply. If you need help, contact the BEL Helpline, 0800–88 22 00. If the disabled person has or gets money or property which takes them out of Income Support entitlement, they can still get SDA.

(iii) Income Support can be claimed by a 16-year-old disabled person in her own right. If she is at school she has to show that she would be unlikely to get a job within the next year because of her disability. If she has savings above a certain limit, she will not be entitled to

Income Support. You need to check details with your local advice centre, the *Disability Rights Handbook*, and so forth. Claim for both SDA and Income Support. If your child receives SDA, she may then qualify for a top-up to bring her income to the Income Support level. You claim on a separate form for Income Support. Get the leaflet from the post office and send off for the application form using the coupon; or phone the Benefits Enquiry Line and ask for a postal claim form. If you claim by phone, write a short note to confirm your claim; date it and include your name and address; keep a copy; you can get a free stamped addressed envelope from the Post Office. Return the completed claim form within a month or you may lose benefit. The form is long; get advice before completing it. Keep a copy of your completed form in case it gets lost.

(iv) Disability Premium or Severe Disability Premium can be claimed by disabled people who receive Income Support. People with profound intellectual and multiple disabilities can qualify for the Severe Disability Premium if:

(a) They claim Income Support (IS).

(b) They get DLA care component at the middle or higher rate.

(c) No one gets Invalid Care Allowance for looking after them.

(d) They technically count as 'living alone'.

The rules for claiming either premium, but especially Severe Disability Premium, are very complicated; they are set out in detail in the *Disability Rights Handbook*. An example may help to illustrate the circumstances in which a disabled person may get it. When Kathy and her friend moved into their Independent Living Project, they claimed SDA and Income Support top-up for their living expenses. They both got Constant Attendance Allowance (now this would be DLA at the higher or middle rate). No one received ICA for looking after them, as their 24-hour care was provided by Crossroads workers, paid by council and Independent Living money. They counted as 'living alone' despite their 24-hour care, because they were tenants of their council home, even though the tenancy was underwritten by their parents. They occupied the tenancy jointly, and neither was dependant on the other, nor were they close relatives. They claimed Severe Disability Premium and it was awarded to each of them, as they satisfied the rules in the ways listed above.

You apply by completing the Income Support form – phone the DSS Freeline or get one from your local Benefits Agency office; or get the Income

Support leaflet from the post office and send the attached label off. Get advice when you apply, as the conditions are so complicated.

4. HOUSING BENEFIT

If you claim Income Support, you will get an application form for Housing Benefit at the same time as you receive the IS claim form. If you want to claim Housing Benefit but do not claim Income Support, you will need to write to the local authority and ask them for an application form. (Address in phone book; look for the name of the area you live in.) Date your letter, include your name and address, keep a copy; if you get benefit, this should be the date it starts.

Housing Benefit is payable to the householder, that is, the person who is 'liable' for the rent. It will not apply to most people with profound intellectual and multiple disabilities unless they are living in the kind of 'independent' situation described earlier.

5. COUNCIL TAX

(i)   You can get help with Council Tax if you are on a low income and have less than £16,000 in savings.

(ii) As a carer, you may be entitled to a discount. Get the leaflet from Carers National Association about this before you apply. They have found that council staff do not always have accurate information, and this may put you off applying unless you are sure of your grounds.

6. BENEFITS TO HELP WITH PAYING FOR ITEMS

(i) The Family Fund

This is funded by the government. Families caring for a 'severely mentally or physically handicapped' child under the age of 16 can apply for a grant for an item they need to help with the care of the child. You usually apply for things not normally provided by the local council or health authority. Examples could be a washing machine for someone who is incontinent; extra bedding, clothing, footwear if they wear out more quickly than usual because of the disability.

You apply by writing to the Family Fund (PO Box 50, York YO1 2ZX); ask for an application form, and the booklet explaining how they might help. A Family Fund social worker will visit you to discuss your application. There is no means test; however, they will consider your income and social circumstances when making a decision. If you are refused, appeal by re-applying; give more or new evidence to back your application. If you are refused again, you can appeal to the Management Committee of the Fund. You should get advice before going to this stage.

(ii) The Social Fund

This is another complicated one. There are various grants under this heading, and you should get advice before sending in your application. There are more details in the *Disability Rights Handbook*; anyone advising you should be using the *Social Fund Officer's Guide*, but bear in mind that local social fund officers have a lot of say in decisions.

I shall concentrate on the Community Care Grants, which may be applicable to someone with profound intellectual and multiple disabilities. (The information leaflet and application form are available from your local Benefits Agency office.) They can be:

(a) Payments to help people move out of institutions into the community or to avoid going into institutional care. An example could be a grant to help with the expenses of setting up home.

(b) Payments to help families cope with exceptional pressures. Examples might be for specialist furniture, bedding or a washing machine for someone who is incontinent.

If the disabled person has savings above certain limits, they will be expected to contribute towards the items. Check the current limits.

There is no legal right to grants from the Social Fund. If the local budget runs out, you may be refused while someone in the next area gets a grant.

If you are refused, or think the amount is too low, you can ask for a review; you must do this in writing, to the social fund officer, at your local DSS office. If you are turned down again, you will be offered an interview. You can take a representative, and put forward your case. Take any further or fresh evidence. The officer will ask you if you agree to the record (s)he makes of the interview; do not sign unless you agree. If you are still refused, a more senior officer will take details of the interview and consider your case. If they refuse you, ask for a further review within 28 days of the first one. The social fund inspector will then be sent all the papers and will consider your case. If you are still unsuccessful, you can apply for a judicial review. You should be taking advice all through this process. As usual, keep copies of all forms you fill in and all papers, letters and so on, you send or receive.

7. HELP WITH CARE COSTS

From April 1993 your local Social Services must respond to a request to assess the care needs of people with disabilities, under the 1990 National Health and Community Care Act. For more details, see Chapter 11, Respite and Residential Services.

8. CHRISTMAS BONUS

This will be paid to someone who is receiving certain benefits, including SDA and DLA, as long as they are entitled to them for the week starting with the first Monday in December. It should be included in the order for that week if you have a book, or by Giro or credit transfer, depending on how you receive your payments.

IMPORTANT: DLA AND RESPITE OR HOSPITAL CARE

If a disabled person goes into respite care regularly, they may eventually lose some of the DLA Care Component for some of the days they spend there. They will continue to be entitled to it for the days they spend at home. It is possible to avoid this by working out the pattern of respite care carefully. There is clear guidance in the *Disabilities Rights Handbook* on how to do this. Briefly, once the disabled person has had 28 days of respite care, either all at once or added up over several week, DLA Care Component will then not be paid for any further days of respite care unless:

1. The disabled person spends the next 29 days in her own home; then she can start building up a fresh 28 days.

2. The disabled person has, for example, 14 weekends going in to respite care on Friday and returning home on Monday; and then for the next four weekends goes in Saturday and returns home on Sunday. This is because the days of going in to and leaving respite care do not count. For the following 14 weekends she can then have Friday to Monday without losing benefit.

If you cannot manage either pattern, you may need to send the book back and go for credit transfer payment for the days the disabled person spends at home. Always let the DLA Unit know, in writing, the dates the person you care for goes into and leaves respite care. If you are able to plan a regular pattern, give them the details in advance.

DLA Care Component will continue to be paid for the first 28 days a disabled person is in hospital; this is 84 days for children under 16. There are rules for adding up days from separate stays within certain periods. See the *Disability Rights Handbook* for details.

THE RIGHTS OF THE DISABLED PERSON

There are two important points to remember:

1. Any benefits you claim on behalf of a person with disabilities belong to them, and should be used for their needs. The only exceptions are ICA and the Carer's Premium.

2. If the disabled person over 16 cannot manage their benefits the carer can apply to become their Appointee. The Appointee makes claims, receives or collects payments, manages the person's finances and deals with enquiries and correspondence. There is a leaflet available from your local Benefits Agency office explaining how to do this. Fill it in and send it off; someone will call round to see you and the disabled person together.

FURTHER INFORMATION

Carers National Association, 20/26 Glasshouse Yard, London EC1A 4JS. Tel: 071–490–8818. Carersline: 071–490–8898. Leaflets on benefits for people with disabilities and their carers; advice on how to claim.

Contact-A-Family, 170 Tottenham Court Road, London W1P 0HA. Contact Helpline: 071–383–3555. Advice, activities, local groups, contacts for children with the same condition. Fact Sheet: Child Disability Benefits and Other Sources of Help.

DSS Freephones:

DSS Freeline: 0800–666–555 – general advice or information.

BEL (Benefits Enquiry Line): 0800–88–22–00 – advice on disability benefits; form completion service.

Disability Living Allowance Unit, Warbreck House, Warbreck Hill, Blackpool FY2 0YE. Tel: 0345–123456.

Family Fund, PO Box 50, York, YO1 2ZX. Tel: 0904–62 11 15. Financial help to families caring for severely handicapped children.

MENCAP, Royal Society for Mentally Handicapped Children and Adults, 117–123 Golden Lane, London EC1Y 0RT. Tel: 071–454–0454. Leaflet with details of benefits.

RADAR, The Royal Association for Disability and Rehabilitation, 12 City Forum, 250 City Road, London EC1V 8AF. Tel: 071–250–3222. Information, advice and publications on all aspects of disability needs, benefits, etc.

Spastics Society, 12 Park Crescent, London W1N 4EQ. Tel: 071–636–5020. Helpline: 0800–62 62 16. Advice, fact sheets, publications.

Publications

Disability Rights Handbook: The Disability Alliance Educational and Research Association, Universal House, 88–94 Wentworth Street, London E1 7SA. Tel: 071–247–8776. This has full details of all benefits relevant to people with disabilities; it explains how to apply and how to appeal if you are refused. It sets out in detail the conditions for receiving the benefits. It has lists of useful addresses, local law centres and other advice centres. An updated edition is published every April.

The National Welfare Benefits Handbook and the Rights Guide to Non-Means Tested Benefits: from CPAG, 1–5 Bath Street, London EC1V 9PY. Tel: 071–253–3406. Full information on all benefits, regularly up-dated.

Part Five

Doctors and Hospitals

CHAPTER 16

YOUR GP

Whether a disabled person is at home with carers or is in residential accommodation, they should be registered with the local GP. The relationship with the GP is very important. Most GPs will see very few, if any, people with profound intellectual and multiple disabilities. If we were moving house or the GP in the practice changed, we made an appointment to see the new one while Kathy was well, so they could see her as she normally was. As well as establishing the new relationship for Kathy, this meant it was easier for the doctor later to judge how far there was cause for concern, knowing what was normal for her.

You should be able to feel that the GP is someone you can go to first if you are concerned. When you are caring for someone with multiple disabilities who may not communicate easily and may have other complicated conditions, it is important, when she is not her usual self, to be able to have quick access to a doctor who can check the obvious possibilities – checking temperature, pulse, blood pressure; listening to the chest, checking ears, throat and so on. If all that draws a blank, a GP who has made an effort to get to know the disabled person will be able to use that knowledge and their experience to talk through with you other possibilities. If the GP feels there is cause for concern they can, depending on the urgency, call an ambulance, arrange for you to be seen at a hospital with a view to admission, or decide on other possible courses of action.

During the last twelve years of Kathy's life we found her GPs very ready to see her at short notice and without appointment if we expressed concern. They were genuinely interested and caring, and very thorough, and would have a good go at sorting the problem out before passing it on. We also found that the practice receptionists took a warm interest in Kathy and took a lot of trouble to sort out any difficulties, for example with prescriptions. Our experience before this was less happy. We usually felt in this earlier period that the doctors were finding it hard to deal with Kathy, and as no real relationship was built up, they had little to offer. During those years we tended to go straight to hospital casualty, which was more traumatic for Kathy if she was unwell, and should not have been necessary just to try and sort out whether she had an infection or other problem and to decide on treatment.

The only real problem in recent years arose if Kathy became ill out of surgery hours, especially at night or over the weekend. The practice used a locum service, and although they were very efficient and always got someone to us fast, the doctors who arrived varied enormously in their ability to cope with sorting out Kathy's disabilities from what we were describing as her current problems.

You are likely also to need your GP to obtain regular medication and other supplies on prescription. In addition, GPs are the key to contact with a range of services and can be helpful in gaining access to some facilities, for example obtaining a wheelchair, or getting help with caring. They may have to write letters or sign forms confirming disability for some benefits, exemptions from some charges, and so on.

When Kathy transferred from the children's to the adult hospital, it was difficult at first to get a consultant to accept her. Children's hospitals and paediatricians are usually able to cope with someone who has more than one condition, but in an adult hospital you have to be put into a specialist compartment; for each doctor you are the 'epilepsy' or the 'joint problems'. At that time Kathy's outstanding problem was her bowel condition, so the GP contacted a gastroenterologist at the local hospital and arranged for a home visit. This began the professional relationship soundly especially from Kathy's point of view, as she first met him on her home ground and was less passive and more confident in interacting. From his point of view his first contact with Kathy was with her relaxed and playing in her own home, not as more usually, passive in her wheelchair in clinical surroundings. He was therefore able in future when he saw her to judge how she was in comparison with her 'best self'. Just as important, he was more likely to view her as a person in her own right and not just as a bundle of problems.

Another way in which the GP was able to help was when we were planning to travel abroad with Kathy.He would write a letter stating that Kathy was not travelling against medical advice, to comply with the terms of the holiday insurance for someone with a disability. He briefly described her condition, listed her medication, and included a note about some of the special medical items we had to carry in case there were any problems at customs. There is an example of a similar letter in Chapter 20, Leisure Activities.

If you are not satisfied with your GP, be clear about the reasons. You will not always agree, especially if the issues are complex. (S)he will not always have the answers, especially if the person you care for is complex. If you feel the doctor is not genuinely interested or not prepared to take the necessary trouble, then you should change. The local Community Health Council will give you a list of other local GPs, and may know of local practices who are especially interested in disabled people. Your best information will be from other parents and carers in the local area. If there is a local voluntary group concerned with disability, they may be able to share information.

A good GP will look upon having someone with multiple disabilities on their list as an opportunity to widen their knowledge and experience. Until medical training offers more than a passing glance at the needs of people with disabilities, this will be the best you can expect.

CHAPTER 17

IN CASUALTY

Most carers of people like Kathy make occasional or even frequent visits to casualty/accident or emergency departments of hospitals.

Once you have visited your local hospital several times, the regular staff will get to know you. It is still useful to have the documentation referred to in Chapters 6, 7 and 9. House doctors will change frequently and may have no experience of treating a person with multiple disabilities.

The following points are useful in ensuring prompt and appropriate treatment:

1. If you are going following a visit to your GP, get her to write a letter explaining the problem, for you to take along.

2. Telephone before arriving if not using an ambulance. Staff will then expect you and you may save waiting time.

3. Have a bag packed at all times with basics you may need for a few hours for example, nappy changes, wipes, drinks, snacks. Include spares of any specialist needs such as catheters, naso-gastric tubes, dressings – the hospital may not have them in the right size, or at all. We used to include some of Kathy's familiar dolls and toys. It is essential to take all current medication. You may be there for hours and it may not be possible to obtain medication in the form normally used or even at all for some less usual drugs. We kept Kathy's medication in a large plastic box with measuring spoons and pots, tablet crusher, and so on.

4. If you arrive by ambulance, you will go straight through. Otherwise, state the problem clearly at reception and be insistent if you feel the situation is dangerous. If we waited a long time and Kathy became more distressed we would ask to be seen more quickly. If we went because of severe fitting and were kept waiting, we would try

reception once more and if there was no response would take her straight in to the casualty ward.

5. We expected doctors and nurses to talk directly to Kathy even though we had to explain the problem to them. We expected they would explain to her what they were doing. If we felt there were difficulties in what they were proposing we suggested how to manage. For example, I always preferred Kathy to sit on my lap while doctors took blood, as I could cuddle and comfort her. X-rays were often difficult as her spine was twisted and she could not lie flat. I usually wore a lead apron and helped to position her with pillows and so forth. Sometimes I had to hold her in place. In many paediatric hospitals or departments staff are more used to this participation. In adult hospitals they are often not, and difficulties are made worse because equipment is often not in small sizes, when sometimes multiply disabled people are.

    If potentially distressing procedures were proposed, such as catheterisation, we would weigh up how ill we felt she was and how essential they were at that stage.

6. We would make sure nurses and doctors listened carefully to our explanation of Kathy's general condition as well as the specific problem.

    Multiply disabled people do not always present the usual symptoms. Sometimes this is because of certain medication. Sometimes it is because the person cannot easily communicate the site of the pain. There seem to be less clearly understood reasons also, in, for example, chest infections – the result can be that the person is actually much more ill than they clinically appear.

    You need to trust your instincts. If you know someone well you know when there is something wrong. Kathy was sometimes found to have pneumonia even though she had no temperature and was not coughing. Kathy's attitude was also that she made an effort every minute she did not actually feel terribly ill. When a doctor arrived she might rouse herself to be sociable, pick up her doll and show it, then smile or laugh; nurses and doctors took this as a sign that she was not too bad and did not see her a few minutes later when she flopped out or became distressed.

    The other common reaction when Kathy was uncommunicative or passive was to assume that because of the multiple disabilities she was like that all the time. It was important to stress that she normally made eye contact, sat up, tried to be sociable, occupied herself, and so on.

7. The doctors you see first are young, relatively inexperienced and often very tired. We were told at the outset of one consultation: 'We haven't got any beds.' Insist on a thorough investigation and say firmly that you are sure they will find a bed if they consider it necessary. We gradually noted all the basic investigations and ran through our own check-list if we felt they were missing anything out.

    If you are not satisfied, ask to see the Senior Medical Registrar. If you are there in the day time, ask for someone from the 'firm' of your regular consultant if you have one, and if it is your usual hospital, or a specialist in that aspect of the condition you are concerned about at the time.

8. Do not leave if you are unhappy. Do not leave until you are sure what has been done, what the doctors think, and have decided whether this agrees with how you see things. If you decide on balance you will return home, even if things have been left very uncertain, be sure on what basis you are going, and state your right to return later if you have further concerns.

    We would sometimes prefer to return home even when Kathy was obviously unwell, as we felt we could make her more comfortable. Our decision was based at that stage on how much specialist care and investigation we felt she needed, as opposed to how much caring care.

9. If medication is prescribed, ask the doctor to check for interactions with other medication. For example, one particular anti-biotic interacts with a particular anti-convulsant to cause deep sleep. Doctors can quickly look this up in the British National Formulary, a copy of which should be easily available to them.

10. Ask nurses and doctors to explain any terms you don't understand. If you have been caring for a while and seem competent and knowledgeable, they may assume you understand all the jargon.

11. If you are out for the day or on holiday, you may need to call in to a casualty department. If you have your basic documentation with you – medication, diary, care book, etc. – it will be easier for staff to take in the full implications of your concern.

Two common reactions we met in this situation were:

(i) Shock, fear, if those staff had not come across someone with such a degree of severe multiple disability before. It could then be difficult for them to understand the difference between the general background problems and the reason why you have come in.

(ii) A failure to understand the potential seriousness of a situation because Kathy seemed to them to be behaving inappropriately, for example, grabbing items, laughing.

You need to be able to state your case clearly and deal with any misunderstandings or muddle. Your diary can be helpful if you need to refer to how frequent symptoms have been, for example, vomiting or fits.

You may be far from home, staying in holiday accommodation or on your way to a destination. You need to consider very carefully the disadvantages of admission to a hospital where the person you care for is not known, and you are far from home, possibly even abroad. These considerations need to be balanced against the possible dangers of travelling with someone who could become very ill. You need to be very clear in your own mind about the doctors' conclusions, and your feelings about these, before agreeing on a course of action.

When travelling abroad with Kathy we tried to obtain details of a suitable local hospital in case of emergency. The consultant sometimes had a professional contact in another country, or some other source of information. If you are travelling in the UK, the local Community Health Council can provide information about hospitals in different areas.

CHAPTER 18

IN HOSPITAL

Sometimes Kathy had a planned admission for investigations or treatment. Sometimes she was admitted from casualty or after referral from the GP.

While Kathy attended the children's hospital, many of her basic needs were attended to as a matter of course, as in principle many of her personal care needs were the same as those of babies and young children. There were many details it was not necessary to check on, such as recording of fluid and food intake, output such as passing of urine, opening of bowels and vomiting, and recording of details and frequency of epileptic fits. For example, management of Kathy's continence was done efficiently because staff were used to dealing with nappies and preventing sore bottoms.

There were issues around her communication of her needs and interpretation of this, and especially around diagnosis of illness when the 'usual signs' were not always present, or she may be reacting a-typically. In the open atmosphere of collaboration between families and professionals these issues could be discussed openly, and there was a willingness to work for a resolution of difficulties. Discussions with nurses, doctors and other staff such as physiotherapists usually took the form of dialogue rather than simply question and answer or being told what was to happen. Kathy's care book was still very important, especially at night and when there were unfamiliar staff or following transfer to another ward.

PARENTS'/CARERS' ANXIETIES

Parents and carers are naturally anxious when the disabled person becomes ill or there is some change in their condition. If this has happened suddenly, this anxiety may be acute. However, they may also have been worrying for weeks while the GP and other doctors have examined her and considered the problems. The discussions referred to above can then become very fraught. Doctors may perceive parents or carers as over-anxious, and fail to listen to important details. Parents or carers may give an impression of anger or hostility, particularly if they feel there has been delay in attending to their concerns about the person they care for. However helpful and understanding the doctor they are seeing may be, that person may receive the accumulated frustration caused by failures further back along the line. It is particularly useful in this situation to have a diary or record which demonstrates the evidence for your concerns.

Once when Kathy had been unwell for some months, gradually losing weight, appetite becoming poor, dreadful watery diarrhoea, we agreed she should go ahead with a planned holiday on the Isle of Wight with her carers. She had been seeing the GP regularly and attending outpatients at the children's hospital, and no cause had yet been found for her current problems. She was nevertheless amazingly cheerful and she and her carers were looking forward to this holiday. They all did their best, and seem to have had a good time for most of the week. Towards the end of the week, however, they telephoned us to say that Kathy had stopped eating and drinking altogether and was vomiting frequently. We agreed that it was better for them to return to London immediately, where she was better known, and we met her and the carers off the train and all went straight to the children's hospital. Kathy looked dreadful physically, much thinner and showing signs of dehydration, but she was pleased to see us and quite happy to be in the hospital, where she felt secure and confident. She showed pleasure at her interactions with doctors and nurses, giggled and laughed. It was the weekend and she saw duty doctors. She was still refusing all food and drink, and we suggested she might be lightheaded as a result, and insisted we felt she really was very ill. It still took twenty-four hours before she was put on a drip, while oral feeds were tried and refused. By then she was very poorly and it soon became clear she had suffered a massive flare-up of her bowel condition. Following tests, she was in hospital for a total of nine months before she was stable enough to leave, and that was using a naso-gastric tube. Our conviction that she was indeed very ill came over as anxiety and it was possibly felt we were over-reacting. Once she saw doctors and nurses who knew her, they could see the difference and reacted promptly.

IN THE ADULT HOSPITAL

Once Kathy was transferred to an adult hospital, on her first admission we found we had to communicate her requirements in much more detail. We could no longer take anything for granted.

Essential First Steps

Because this was the first time that Kathy had been admitted to an adult hospital, we were surprised when we arrived on the ward with her to find nurses ready to whisk her away to her bed space and leave us in the waiting room. We had to insist that we accompanied her so that her needs were established right at the outset.

1. CHECK ON BED ARRANGEMENTS

We had to make sure that there were bed sides, and that any spaces between them and the bed were made safe with pillows. We had to check that a waterproof and cotton draw sheet were in place. We had to ask for a ripple bed or similar to be ordered because Kathy was likely to spend more time in bed than other patients and was in danger of developing bed sores. We made sure staff realised that she should never be left even momentarily with the bed sides down, or she would fall or slide out.

2. MAKE SURE THE LOCKER, MEDICATION, EQUIPMENT AND SO FORTH, WAS OUT OF REACH

Even when she was unwell, Kathy would take an interest in her surroundings. She particularly liked blood pressure equipment, oxygen lines, hospital notes and the contents of locker tops, which included medicine pots, instruments, cotton wool, and so on. She would reach into the pockets of nurses and doctors and remove pens, instruments and notes. Notes would be examined and then shredded.

3. HELP TO CARRY OUT PROCEDURES, MAKE TREATMENT AND FEEDING ARRANGEMENTS, AND SO FORTH.

Sometimes Kathy had to have an intravenous line inserted for medication or feeding; sometimes she was tube fed from an overhead bottle. At times she had a combination of lines and tubes. We had to assess her condition and judge whether she was likely to interfere with any of these. If so, we might suggest splinting her arms or similar arrangements. While someone was with her we would release her arms and hands and let her play. It was very restricting but less distressing than having to have lines or tubes replaced more frequently than necessary. Eventually she would accept these arrangements, after understandable protests. Without them, she would not have been able to continue such treatment.

4. CHECK MEDICATION

It was vital to check that medication had been recorded correctly. In a busy hospital it is easy for mistakes to be made in dosages and frequency, especially where the medication list is long and complex. We quickly learned that if an item was not written up it would not be given. Creams and other items had to be written up so that when Kathy's own supplies ran out the hospital could supply them. Timing of drugs was important. Kathy's medication was timed in such a way as to interfere with a normal day as little as possible. Lunch-time medication was kept to a minimum so that she could have a day out without carers having to make elaborate arrangements at midday. We had arrived at the timing of some drugs such as anticonvulsants and pain relief through long experience of what worked best for Kathy. Without any intervention on our part, hospital staff would time drugs as they thought best. We appreciated that on a busy ward Kathy had to fit into established routines but we would make our case strongly in an attempt to arrive at an agreed compromise.

5. NOTIFY SPECIAL DIETARY REQUIREMENTS

It is astonishing that hospital staff do not take diets more seriously. Many people with multiple disabilities have complex allergies or sensitivities. Many chronic illnesses are alleviated by careful attention to diet. It seems to be more generally accepted that where there is a definite medical condition known to require a diet, such as coeliac condition, diabetes or kidney failure, provision of an appropriate diet will be taken more seriously. Even then, the arrangements can break down because of inefficiency and misunderstanding, especially on the ward.

We arrived at a suitable diet for Kathy after years of observation and trial and error. If adhered to, this diet saved her much pain and discomfort. We always took details in to the ward and tried to see the dietician. It usually took at least twenty-four hours for a diet to be organised, and it was impossible to see a dietician and therefore to organise anything if admission was at the weekend. We often took prepared food in. Even when the diet had been agreed, it seemed difficult for all those involved to grasp the principles. Some food and drinks are often given out by domestic staff and they are not aware of dietary requirements. Special diets, even when labelled by name often disappear by the time the trolley has reached your bed, especially if they look more attractive than the usual offer. If the person requiring the diet does not communicate verbally, they may be given food which is unsuitable or even damaging. There were many such instances when Kathy was in hospital, including such examples as giving Weetabix and milk when she was on a low residue and dairy free diet, offering cups of tea, thinking any sandwich would do when the one specially ordered was the only one with dairy free margarine.

6. INVOLVEMENT OF CARERS

We were used to seeing to many of Kathy's needs on the ward during her time at the children's hospital, and had to establish that this would need to happen at the adult hospital. One of us might wish to stay overnight if Kathy was very ill or uncomfortable. Staff were always very helpful in this respect. While we were with Kathy on the ward we were always willing to see to her personal needs, such as changing nappies, giving feeds and medication, bathing and so on, especially when nursing staff were hard pressed. This was often a learning situation for us all, including the other patients. Once when one of us was checking Kathy's charts at the foot of the bed, another patient called out to the sister to 'report' us! It was clearly a sensitive issue when Kathy's father or a male carer was using ward facilities to bathe her, although this has become less of an issue since in recent years more and more wards seem to be mixed. We also had to establish that while we would be very considerate to other patients on the ward, we did expect to be able to visit and attend to Kathy very flexibly. If she was very unwell and we had gone home for a few hours, possibly to eat and shower, we expected to be able to come back even at a late hour to see for ourselves how she was.

Kathy was also cared for by workers at the various residential units she stayed at, and in later years by her own Crossroads (Care Attendant Scheme) workers. We had to discuss this with ward staff and establish that they would be taking their share of seeing to Kathy's personal needs, socialising with her, and so on.

However, striking the right balance in all this was essential. Anyone new to caring for Kathy got to know her and to communicate with her through attending to her personal needs. There was always so much to be done and these routines were so important for Kathy's well-being and comfort, that the interactions resulting soon enabled a relationship to develop. Kathy was always very appreciative if things were being done properly, and she expressed her appreciation in a very direct way. Once the communication was established carers could then easily learn about her personal tastes and wishes in activities. It was therefore always important for nursing staff to do their share of caring for Kathy as through this they would get to know her in the same way. Only if they could quickly establish some knowledge of her and a degree of communication could they tell if she became more ill or if something was wrong.

THE ADMISSION INTERVIEW WITH THE DOCTOR

Once the nursing staff have settled their patient into the ward, or at some point while they are doing all this, the doctor will arrive to carry out the admission interview. This is usually the house doctor for the ward, relatively young and inexperienced and often very tired and harassed from working long hours. This interview is very important to establish the basis on which the patient will be approached.

The actual scope of the interview will vary according to whether this is a planned admission or the result of an emergency. The doctor will often want to go briefly over the patient's history from birth. This can be difficult, especially if you are really worried about the condition of the person you care for and feel the doctor should be getting on with the treatment. However, it is your opportunity to set the person with the disabilities in a proper context, to highlight important events in their lives in terms of their condition and above all to give a clear picture of how they are when they are not so unwell. You can demonstrate by your own attitude how you expect medical and nursing staff to address and deal with the person you care for, for example by addressing them directly and involving them in discussions about their likely treatment. You will need to double check medication, especially if the list is lengthy. You will need to reinforce all the points made above about requirements and your involvement and that of other carers. When patients are admitted, a treatment plan is drawn up, and you will want to ask what this is and be clear about what is proposed. Ask when the ward rounds take place, when the consultant comes round to see each patient, so that you can be there.

THE TWO KEY ISSUES

Once the basics had been established, which was often quite time consuming and exhausting for all concerned, we then found that there were two essential issues when someone like Kathy was in hospital.

Communicating her Value as a Person

This still seems to be a difficult issue for some hospital staff, especially some doctors. At a very basic level I am talking about the right of people like Kathy to be valued as someone with full rights to consideration of their needs and options for treatment. Even though Kathy would never earn her own living or contribute directly to the gross national product, we always insisted that she had full rights in all respects and should be valued for the contribution she did make at many levels.

I have referred in a previous chapter to common reactions of some doctors on meeting someone with Kathy's range and degree of disability. Some were obviously shocked and afraid, unable to reach behind the clinical picture to the very real person there. They assumed when they saw her unwell or recovering from severe fitting that she was always like that. This might then lead them to feel that not much could be done and to limit their options for investigation and treatment. Some doctors, on seeing her, appeared to consign her immediately to a 'subnormal' category, either making false assumptions about her humanity, or more crudely, considering her of less value than 'normal' people. This, in turn, could lead to a failure to consider the full range of options for investigation and treatment on the grounds that she did not deserve that full consideration. Some felt upset and sorry, especially if they saw her very ill and distressed. One doctor described her in a letter to another as a 'poor girl'. This also limited their view of what was possible for Kathy, as they did not see beyond this view to the real person who might be in pain and discomfort, but was strong in her resolve to be herself and whose determination could be harnessed to help her recover.

We always spoke to Kathy about any diagnosis and about any proposed procedures, for example insertion of an intravenous line or tube. We expected nurses and doctors to address her directly. We were never sure exactly how much she understood, but she certainly tried to make sense of what was happening to her and deserved all the clues we could give her. Without this it is even more frightening to be approached by strangers who stick things into you, pull you about, put you in or under strange machines, and inevitably hurt you at times.

It was very important for Kathy to have as many familiar things and experiences as possible in such a potentially disturbing environment. We would take in her favourite objects, so she could occupy herself when no one was there to give her personal attention. Staff had to learn to value these things as much as she did, so that if they disappeared we all thought it important to track them down, and if they got soiled we all made sure they were saved to be cleaned.

One of Kathy's passions was music, but not just any music; she had very definite tastes. When a doctor saw us once, he read through a recent letter from me about Kathy's progress, and noticed that I had mentioned that she liked much classical music but not some composers such as Schoenberg. He asked me with obvious scepticism if I was serious. I replied that I was absolutely serious, that Kathy knew the difference between various styles of music, had likes and dislikes as did we all, and that it made her unhappy to listen to music she disliked.

We realised that when Kathy was in hospital she could not be bathed in sound as at home, with music filling the room; the other patients on an open ward would have their own tastes and rights in what they preferred to listen to. If Kathy was not in an individual room, we would rig up a tape player to the mains and persuade her to accept earphones; if she used a personal stereo she got through a lot of batteries in a short time.

Once hospital staff realised that Kathy was happier and more settled when she had her usual occupations and pleasures, they would do their best to maintain these things. It was a revelation, especially to doctors who did not know Kathy, to see how she switched from being bored and restless to beaming with pleasure when 'her' music was switched on. Similarly, any old doll would not do, it had to be the current favourite. Unless staff grasped these issues, and took them seriously, they would not know the difference between Kathy in a towering rage because no one would supply the correct item or activity, and Kathy in great distress because she was in pain or discomfort.

In recent years nurses seem more aware of these issues and their practice more frequently reflects this valuing of the person for themselves. Staffing shortages and pressures through lack of resources often prevent them from consistently implementing this good practice.

With doctors, it seems to be more a question of their own personal philosophy and possibly whether they have any personal experience of a person with a disability. There are a hundred and one approaches and attitudes, and the issue is too important to be left to chance. There does seem to be a huge gap in medical training in preparing doctors for this area of work and in dealing with the ethical issues arising from treating very severely disabled people.

Establishing a Correct Diagnosis and Appropriate Intervention

A good doctor looks at and listens to their patient very carefully, as well as carrying out the usual checks and tests. With someone like Kathy, doctors had to listen very carefully to us and her carers to, if they were to build up an accurate picture.

It does seem to be the case that people with severe multiple disabilities do not always present the usual symptoms when they are ill. We certainly found this to be the case with Kathy, but other parents and carers and disabled people who are able to speak for themselves have confirmed this. Some of the reasons for this can be fairly easily worked out, certainly by doctors. If a person is on a complex cocktail of medication, a new drug may interact to cause an unexpected development, such as drowsiness, vomiting, or making one of the other drugs more or less effective. When Kathy was ill in hospital with pneumonia once, she was prescribed the antibiotic considered most effective for the infection she had. Although her chest began to clear she became even more drowsy until eventually she was sleeping for twenty-four hours and could hardly be roused, even by pain. It turned out that this particular antibiotic was reacting with one of her anticonvulsants to produce the drowsiness. This could have easily been checked before prescribing by the doctor checking in the interactions table in the British National Formulary, the book doctors use to check the types of drug to prescribe, their side effects and interactions with other drugs. Once the antibiotic was changed she gradually came round. Had the mistake not been discovered, the consequences could have been very serious as, despite the 'clinical' improvement in her chest infection, the fact that she was lying down all the time and unable to eat and drink orally may well have led to further complications.

Some drugs suppress certain symptoms. Steroids given for a range of conditions will suppress inflammation, temperature, and so on. Kathy was on steroids for many years to treat her rheumatoid arthritis and her bowel disease. Sometimes she became ill with, say, a chest infection, and there was no high temperature, no cough, only a sad person who was sleepy and not herself. Sometimes she had pneumonia with no temperature. Kathy also took aspirin regularly for her rheumatoid arthritis, and this also suppressed a high temperature. She would therefore appear suddenly to become very ill, although in fact the infection had been brewing up for several days. Even though this was common medical knowledge, and in addition she may have had frequent fits, also a possible sign of infection, it was not always picked up quickly by doctors who went by the 'clinical signs', sounding the chest and so on. This could lead to dangerous delays in treatment.

Some of the reasons why people like Kathy are not assessed accurately at first are due to attitudes, referred to earlier, where doctors see someone smiling or perhaps grabbing at things out of curiosity, and jump to the conclusion that there cannot possibly be anything seriously wrong.

Another factor may be that many people with severe disabilities are used to pain and discomfort to a degree most of us could not imagine. They do not always complain as early or as loudly as others who do not normally experience such problems. This may be taken as indicating that it is unlikely that serious illness is present. Kathy was very stoical, having endured years of severe pain and discomfort. When her pain was greater than usual, her first reaction was to become very quiet and withdrawn, pretend to sleep, stop her usual activities, refuse food and drink, allow herself to lie quietly and be cuddled. If Kathy cried or screamed with pain we knew it must be very bad indeed.

There may be other factors as yet not established, which mean that doctors may have to take that much more care with establishing a diagnosis with a disabled person who is clearly not their usual self. It is accepted that children react differently to illness and drugs than adults; it is understood that elderly people may require modification of drug amounts because their bodies are reacting differently. These facts have been established through observation and experience and have passed into medical knowledge. People with severe disabilities deserve the same level of attention to establish the factors that make their response to illness sometimes not the typical one.

When the illness is very serious, prompt diagnosis and appropriate action are crucial. With someone like Kathy who could not communicate verbally, medical indications such as how aware she was were vital. On a busy ward these were not always picked up by staff. Even worse, when these signs were noticed by carer,s they were not always taken seriously and investigated. When someone who is already very fragile is developing a chest infection, for example, an early sign may be a change in how alert and aware they are, their conscious level. If this is not picked up as soon as it is noticed and the person checked and tested for possible causes, valuable time can be lost in treating an infection.

When a diagnosis has been made and treatment begun, there can still be problems. Someone who has severe disabilities may require careful monitoring of food and fluid intake; they may even require tube feeding or feeding through a vein. It seems increasingly the case on busy wards that the attention to detail required to maintain such routines is not possible with the current staffing levels. Things we used to take for granted, such as careful records of intake and output seem no longer to be given such importance. The result can be that when a doctor asks how much nourishment a patient has taken within a given period, or even how much fluid, no one knows the answer. If continuous tube feeding is required, the old fashioned system of giving it from a bottle overhead is very unreliable and needs constant checking and adjusting. Pumps to control delivery of tube feeds should be routine, but we have been in situations where none was available, making feeding an erratic procedure. One result can be that a patient who is already very ill can literally starve.

When a patient's condition becomes critical, doctors need to have an accurate picture of what is happening so that they can examine the options and discuss these with carers. During Kathy's last illness we were in a situation where, as her condition deteriorated rapidly, confirmed by nursing staff and physiotherapists attending her, doctors did not seem to believe the evidence of their own eyes or to take seriously the concern of other staff and carers, but relied mechanically on procedures to make judgements about what to do next. For the reasons given above or for other reasons best known to themselves, doctors then failed to carry out certain procedures which would have checked their observations. They were not in a position then to convey an accurate view of Kathy's condition, and certain treatment options were never considered.

The daughter of friends, with a similar level of disability to Kathy, and also prone to chest infections in recent years, was in another London hospital being treated for pneumonia. She was said to have 'responded' to antiobiotic treatment. It was clear the doctors needed the bed, and her mother was told she was being discharged. Her mother refused, convinced that the infection was still active. She used her observations of the young woman she knew and cared for, not simply routine examinations. Reluctantly, the hospital agreed to keep her for a further day, during which it became clear that the infection was still present, and further treatment was necessary.

There are some important lessons here for doctors, which need disseminating urgently. There are also some important lessons for parents and carers. If you have cared for someone for many years you know them best. If you think something is wrong, you are probably right. I tried very hard over the years to control the outward expression of my anxiety when Kathy was ill, so that I would not appear over-emotional and my representations would be taken more seriously. In our concern to communicate properly with professionals, I think we took this too far in her last years, and perhaps suppressed gut-feelings about her condition which certainly turned out to be correct during her last illness. I was not right on every occasion, but on most. Parents and carers should rely on their knowledge of the disabled person and on their instincts. They should insist that doctors are called if they are worried, or nursing or other staff seem anxious. They should keep asking for more information, express their fears openly and ask what tests and other procedures would normally be carried out. They should jump up and down if necessary, and make a fuss until their concerns are taken seriously.

However, it is the doctors themselves who have to take this on. We found, on what turned out to be Kathy's last day alive, that we were paralysed with fear, unable even to voice our worries about Kathy's condition. When I look back, I wonder why a doctor examining her did not notice her parents' distress and feel there was more cause for concern than his own examination seemed to indicate. We should have been pressed to reveal our worries, not been ignored.

It is Difficult to do the Usual Tests...

When someone is ill with puzzling symptoms it is usual for doctors to think of the most likely possibilities, and then suggest tests to check these. We found sometimes that unless we gave considerable thought to how we could help Kathy to cope with some of these tests, they would have been abandoned or never suggested in the first place.

BLOOD TESTS were not usually a problem, perhaps because Kathy had so many in her life. I would usually hold her on my lap and distract her. The phlebotomists (the technicians who take the blood) were usually very sensitive, chatting to her and taking great care. We found there were problems if an inexperienced doctor was taking blood; perhaps their nervousness communicated itself to Kathy. When she was very ill, there were sometimes problems in actually getting blood out. If this happened I would put her music on if possible, stroke her head, tummy, try to relax her.

URINE TESTS were very difficult, as Kathy was incontinent and wore nappies. It was reasonable for doctors to assume on some of our visits to casualty that she might have a urinary infection when she was obviously unwell and nothing else seemed to be wrong. As the only way to get a clean specimen was by catheter, we rarely agreed to this unless it seemed absolutely essential, for instance if kidney problems were suspected. Kathy found insertion of a catheter distressing, partly because of a slight physical abnormality. When she was being examined at the adult hospital the situation was made worse because they did not have child size catheters.

X-RAYS were obviously not in themselves painful, and if Kathy was not very distressed she often enjoyed the interactions with the radiologist. However, as Kathy got older and her physical disabilities more marked, even routine X-rays became more difficult. She could not stand and her back was not straight. Sometimes she could sit in her wheelchair and have the X-ray plates inserted behind her or held in front. Usually, I found it was better to lie her down on the couch, and prop her with a variety of wedges and pillows. If she needed to lie flat, the only way to get her body flat against the plate was for me to dress up in a lead apron and hold her legs up. Skull X-rays taken after an unexplained injury to her head required me to advise on propping her comfortably and then to stand so she could see me, while I attracted her attention by generally making a fool of myself, so she kept her head still for the time required. She was obviously astonished by my behaviour – but she kept still long enough for the job to be done. Again, in an adult hospital or casualty department equipment and experience will be geared to adult sizes, and a small disabled person is not easily catered for.

EAR, NOSE and THROAT examinations were often quite routine for Kathy, when doctors were checking for causes of distress. These came into the category of me holding her firmly while the doctors did them as quickly as possible. Kathy never liked being restrained in any position, and it was not possible to give her any choice in the matter. She always protested much more than with many more uncomfortable, invasive and even painful tests.

EYE EXAMINATIONS I would dread, because again Kathy hated having her head held still, and protested vigorously when lights were shone in her eyes. One day a small area of blood appeared in one eyeball, and we were worried that she might have knocked herself, or there might be some other problem. It was a Sunday, and we went to the casualty department of the eye hospital. We played and chatted with Kathy to keep her relaxed, although I dreaded her reaction when she saw the doctor. I explained about Kathy's disabilities and learning difficulties before we started, and the doctor was understanding and sensible. Between us we worked out how best she should approach Kathy. We got Kathy to look in different directions by holding her familiar objects up, and singing and calling out to her. In the end a very thorough examination was possible, which confirmed that there was a small haematoma (collection of blood) but its site did not indicate a serious problem and it would gradually disperse. The attitude of the doctor helped considerably here, but I also realised that Kathy was growing up and was becoming more tolerant of some situations provided she felt reasonably secure.

E.E.G. examination involves small electrodes being glued to the scalp so that the brain waves can be monitored. This was usually done with Kathy to monitor her epilepsy. She did not mind the gluing so much, although she wanted to play with the wires. She did object to sitting still for up to an hour. I never found a satisfactory way of resolving this problem. I usually let her relax until I felt she was going to interfere with the test, and then I would hold her firmly, which led to loud protests. The other problem when someone with a learning disability has an E.E.G. is that they are not necessarily able to respond to requests such as to close their eyes or carry out certain physical movements, so that full monitoring of all functions is not possible.

BRAIN SCANS have an important role in monitoring the condition of someone who has complex epilepsy or apparent deterioration in brain function. They were not available when Kathy was young, but she occasionally had one from her mid-teens. It was easier to manage if she was in hospital at the time, because she was not taken down for it until they were ready, and if it was managed very briskly she would be prepared to lie still with a favourite doll for a brief period. It didn't work if we had to go to outpatients and wait for a long time, when she got restless. At that point we could still have managed it if the operator was sensitive to the difficulties and managed things without further delay. Once, the scan was abandoned because the operator took so long trying to get it perfect that Kathy was beginning to sit up and protest. A less than perfect scan taken more quickly would still have given useful information; as it was, she ended up having no scan at all. It is not unusual for patients to be sedated or even to have a general anaesthetic for a scan, but it depends on the general condition of the person. In Kathy's later years a general anaesthetic would not be considered for routine procedures because of possible complications due to her increasing physical deformities and general fragility.

TESTS REQUIRING STARVING

When Kathy was sixteen she began to develop serious problems with her bowel function. Many of the tests required to establish the cause of this and then to monitor her condition required clearing out the system and starvation, sometimes for up to two days. She was usually in hospital during this preliminary period, so checks could be carried out and to ensure she really was adhering to the instructions. On an open ward this was very difficult to manage. Kathy worked out years ago that when she was in hospital food came on a trolley. She looked out for it to arrive and listened for the clatter of plates and cutlery. She watched for her place to be laid on the bedside table. If she did not have a place, or if no food was served to her but was taken to other patients, she would protest loudly. We would explain this and if possible ask for Kathy to be allocated a separate room. Then at least she didn't have the distraction of meals being served.

After the first few hours, unless she was very ill, she would begin to feel hungry and thirsty and would look at us expectantly. We found we had to stay with her during waking hours to keep her occupied, with plenty of music and activities to take her mind off being empty. If possible we would take her out for walks in the hospital grounds, or further afield in between checks and tests. If Kathy had to stay on an open ward during such a period we always arranged to take her out of the way while meals were being served, even if it was only to walk around the hospital corridors This was less satisfactory, because we mistimed it sometimes, or we would see food trollies in the corridor and Kathy would get agitated.

During the actual tests one of us would go in with her, to give advice on positioning and to hold her hand and talk to her, even if she was sedated.

DENTAL TREATMENT

I have included this under being in hospital, because this is where Kathy got most of her dental treatment, and this is where many of the carers I know have to take the disabled person they care for to obtain treatment. When Kathy was young I tried our local dentist; she would not open her mouth and when the dentist put his finger in her mouth she bit it. This did not make for a fruitful relationship. She had more urgent medical problems which made dental treatment seem less important, and a few years later her teeth needed serious attention. We took her for some years to a special dental clinic at one hospital, where she had a light general anaesthetic in the chair and had a check, scale and polish and any extractions or fillings. After one session she took much longer to come round than previously, and after that she was admitted as an in-patient with provision for an overnight stay afterwards if there were problems. After one annual session when she was about 24, we were told it was too risky for her to have any more general anaesthetics for routine treatment, and only if there was an emergency or she was in severe pain would they contemplate it.

The next year, without much optimism, I took her along to the local community health centre clinic. The surroundings were dingy but there was a couch that moved up and down. The dentist was obviously taken aback to meet Kathy and clearly did not treat many people like her, but he spoke to her directly and cheerfully, and told her what he was doing. With a combination of moving the couch, which fascinated her, and talking her through the various activities, we were all able to co-operate so that the dentist was able to check and clean and scale. It taught me a lesson, which was not to assume Kathy would not be able to change her attitude to certain things. She was continuing to grow up and develop, and when she felt more confident with what was happening she was less likely to protest and more able to give it a try.

DISCHARGE FROM HOSPITAL

When you are told that the person you care for is about to be discharged after tests or treatment, be satisfied in your own mind before you agree. If she was in for treatment, have the doctors achieved what they set out to do? If not, what are the next steps? Is she well enough to come home? Will you need extra help at home for the period after she is discharged?

If she came in for tests, what are the results? If they are not ready yet, have you got an appointment to get them, or how else will you hear? Once you have the results, what are the options for care and treatment?

When you are ready to accept discharge, check the following things:

1. Have there been any changes in medication?

2. If so, have you got supplies of anything new to take home? (Local chemists may need to order some less usual items.)

3. Check all medication and dosages you are given very carefully. We found mistakes were sometimes made when people were busy.

4. Has transport been arranged if you need it?

5. Have you got a follow-up appointment? If not, will one be sent to you?

6. Have you got any special equipment that is needed? If not, when will you get it and who will arrange it?

7. If you need extra help at home, who is arranging it and when will it start?

8. Have you been told what to do and whom to contact if the person you care for does not improve or there are any further problems?

After discharge or in between out-patients appointments, you must feel able to contact the doctor in charge if you have worries. If discharge was very recent, you can telephone the ward. Otherwise, you can get in touch with the doctor in charge by contacting his secretary. She can then pass on a message and the doctor can contact you. You can also ask for the registrar or the house doctor to be bleeped and speak to them directly for advice. If you feel you need an earlier outpatients appointment, do not hesitate to get in touch with the consultant's secretary and ask for this to be arranged.

If you have a good GP they will be able to advise you when you are concerned, but if it is a highly specialised matter you may need advice directly from the hospital.

HOW COULD THINGS BE IMPROVED?

The first step, which cannot be taken for granted, is to assume that people with multiple disabilities will receive all the usual medical services and checks that anyone would who is not disabled. Doctors and other hospital staff must be prepared to be creative in making arrangements for tests. Staff in children's wards and hospitals have valuable experience to offer, as they have had to do this with children too young to understand what is happening to them. The fact that it is going to be more difficult to carry out a particular test should not mean that the test does not take place. Careful attention to details such as arrangement of equipment, especially during serious illness or after operations, can make it less likely that lines will be pulled out, dressings pulled off, or other procedures disrupted. It may be that on a busy ward it will be necessary to allocate a nurse for a period to stay with the patient until they are less distressed or more accustomed to some of the procedures.

New technology often means tests are less unpleasant, but they still usually require the patient to keep still and often to follow instructions. One of the biggest problems for people with profound intellectual and multiple disabilities which include epilepsy, is accurate monitoring of fit activity when fits seem to be changing or getting worse. I have referred earlier to the difficulties with EEGs and brain scans. MRI (magnetic resonance imaging) scans are more sophisticated but still need the patient's co-operation in keeping still for quite a long period. Whole-head MSI (magnetic source imaging) systems still in the research stage should be available in the future. Their big advantage is that they give a picture of electrical activity in the brain as it is happening, and can be done quickly.

Waiting around is one of the biggest problems for people with a significant intellectual disability. Hospital staff may have no idea of how exhausting and difficult the journey has been, and how the return journey is dreaded. The disabled person and their carer may have had to get up very early to be ready in time. It may not be easy to get appropriate food and drink in the hospital. When Kathy was waiting for long periods in outpatients she got very bored because she could not engage in her usual activities, and who knows what fear and apprehension she felt from earlier memories. By the time we got in to see a doctor, or the dentist, or to have the test, she might be raging and screaming, which hardly made for a useful consultation. Again, we noticed that as she got older she got more tolerant of this situation. As with food and meals, she had learned that it was customary to sit about for long periods in hospital outpatients and would be more amenable to occupation and conversation to pass the time. It still depended on how she felt, and if she was in pain and discomfort, sitting for long periods in her wheelchair was not helpful, and she would be very cross and physically restless by the time we went in to see the doctor.

Amenities at the hospital are not always appropriate for the disabled person. Specially adapted lavatories turn out to be not so accessible. I had to ask for a private place where I could change Kathy's nappy, and had to make the best of whatever was offered, sometimes just a floor. If Kathy had fits, it was not always easy to find somewhere private for her to recover. Even in modern hospitals, waiting areas are cramped and do not take account of wheelchairs in the seating spaces. We have had to stand around with Kathy in her wheelchair for long periods in a crowded clinic. One of Kathy's conditions required careful monitoring of her weight. Because she was relatively small and light even as an adult, I could lift her on to the weighing chair, or even stand on the scales with her and then be weighed myself and have my weight subtracted. This would not have been possible with a larger and heavier person. Transport is a problem. Transport is not provided as of right for the disabled person to hospital. When we did obtain it, we found that we had to be up at the crack of dawn in case of an early call, and then might wait for hours to be picked up. If we did not wait around at home for hours, an early pick up meant long hours at the hospital. When everyone was tired after consultations and tests, there was more waiting around. Sometimes the ambulance did not turn up at all. Sometimes we were picked up so late that the clinic had finished by the time we got to the hospital. As a result, we tried to make our own way. This is very difficult in central London, as parking, even special disabled parking, is very difficult. Sometimes I had to be dropped off with Kathy while her father drove round for long periods looking for a parking space. Sometimes it was simpler to get a taxi, which was fine with a small Kathy and a small wheelchair, but not necessarily suitable for all disabled people.

Many people with profound intellectual and multiple disabilities, and their carers, spend a good deal of time in hospitals. If some of the problems discussed above were addressed, that time would be less distressing and exhausting, and would be used more effectively to meet the needs of the patient.

CHAPTER 19

THINGS CAN ONLY GET BETTER…

We used this phrase with caution. Meant as a cheerful encouragement when times were hard, it did not always turn out to be true.

Some things did get better. For Kathy, even though her physical problems increased, she learned to give and receive affection, to form warm relationships, to enjoy and learn from new experiences and to communicate her needs more effectively. For us, we learned to interpret Kathy's needs more accurately and gained expertise in getting the provision to meet those needs. We found out more about her rights and became more powerful in fighting for them. We made good friends who were in similar circumstances, and gained strength from working and fighting with them. We gave support when friends were at the end of their tether, and we received it when we were really down. We discovered skills and strengths we never knew we possessed, and we saw that Kathy was able to teach us and others many truths about ourselves.

And some people with profound intellectual and multiple disabilities remain in good health or improve. Life is still busy but can offer pleasure and satisfaction.

But some get worse. The disabilities themselves or the consequences, such as using a wheelchair, lead to spinal problems. Pain and discomfort follow, braces or operations may be needed. Chest infections may be more likely, and may be life-threatening. Difficulties with sight or hearing may develop or become more severe. Skin is more prone to soreness and infection. Severe epilepsy may lead to further brain damage. Feeding problems may increase and naso-gastric or stomach tubes may be necessary. Urinary and kidney infections may mean catheters have to be used.

Other conditions may appear. At the age of four Kathy had cerebral palsy and severe learning disabilities, and it was difficult to communicate with and relate to her. However, she was just about walking, feeding herself, using a potty and had a few words. At the age of four and a half, out of the blue, she developed rheumatoid arthritis. Suddenly, she was not just severely disabled but seriously ill. The deformities resulting from her arthritis meant she never walked again, and hip and spine problems made sitting up increasingly difficult. The awful pain and continued discomfort made her moody and even more withdrawn, and she quickly lost some of the skills she had taken so long to learn.

She developed a skin condition, vitiligo, where patches lost their pigment. She had to wear sun screen even in winter or the patches burned; in summer great care was needed to avoid blistering and burning.

At ten years old, tremors which we had noticed developed into grand mal epilepsy, and she began to experience many different types of fit, some life threatening.

When the arthritis seemed to have settled a little, and her health picked up, at the age of sixteen she began to have symptoms of what later turned out to be a serious bowel disorder. This gave her more pain and discomfort, with frequent severe diarrhoea. This was hard work to deal with, caused loss of appetite, and eventually resulted in her needing a naso-gastric tube all the time.

Medication for various conditions can cause problems. Steroids make infection more likely to creep up unnoticed, can cause brittle bones and other major problems. Anti-inflammatory drugs can cause problems with the digestive system. Anti-convulsants can cause rashes, liver problems or behaviour disturbances with some people. Some drugs react with others, and this can be dangerous.

There may be long stays in hospital and frequent emergencies. The person you care for may become very fragile generally – you may have more work, more worry and more sadness.

Families caring for people with severe disabilities are more likely to be short of money than others. There are hidden costs such as extra wear and tear on clothing and in the home. Travelling is more complicated and expensive. There may be regular hospital visiting, causing more expense and special arrangements. Special diets may be needed. Special benefits only go a small way to meeting these costs.

AND THE PERSON YOU CARE FOR MAY DIE

Many people who care for those with profound intellectual and multiple disabilities face this possibility constantly. It nearly happens in so many crises, and yet you are never adequately prepared. I know parents to whom this has happened suddenly, and others like us where the person for whom we cared became more and more frail over a period of time, until they almost seemed too tired to make the effort to go on living.

When Kathy died, we felt utter despair at the prospect of life without her. We were angry that her last days in hospital had not been managed better, and that we were not prepared for her approaching death. We miss her for many things, but most of all for the joy she brought to everyday life, turning a simple outing into a memorable experience with her spontaneous delight, lighting up a gloomy day with some piece of mischief and her wicked laughter.

Family, friends and counsellors have helped us to live with this grief, but we and our lives have been fundamentally changed. We do remember the happy times, and it is good to know how many people loved and learned from Kathy. We like to talk about her, and we have kept some of her things. We remember her always, but make special occasions of her birthday, and the anniversary of her death.

We found some books which helped us to work things out in our minds. I have listed some titles at the end of the chapter.

I have written briefly in Chapter 22 about how important the funeral and the farewell ceremonies are. It is also essential that hospital staff learn how to deal with people who do not communicate verbally and may have complex disabilities, and with their carers. To do this, they need to value them. Medical training has to take this issue on, as our children grow up into adults who are increasingly cared for within the community.

Some things could certainly get better if some of the obvious difficulties could be removed:

- If medical and hospital services were more sensitive to the needs of people with profound intellectual and multiple disabilities,

- If local authorities were better at knowing the numbers and needs of disabled people and looked ahead and planned accordingly,

- If lack of money did not always seem to be the main reason for not doing what is necessary,

- If many of the services already touched on in this book were more effective and perceptive.

FURTHER INFORMATION

All in the End is Harvest, an anthology for those who grieve. Edited by Agnes Whitaker. Darton, Longman and Todd/Cruse. (1984). ISBN: 0 232 51624 3.

The Bereaved Parent by Harriet Sarnott Schiff. Souvenir Press. (1979).

Letters to a Younger Son by Christopher Leach. Dent (1981). A father writing about the death of his older son.

Listen to Me by Susannah Kahtan and Pat Fitton, *British Medical Journal* Vol. 307 28/8/93. Discusses medical attitudes to people with complex disabilities.

Storymaking in Bereavement by Alida Gersie. Jessica Kingsley Publishers (1991). ISBN: 1 85302 065 6.

Part Six

Making My life Worthwhile

CHAPTER 20

LEISURE ACTIVITIES

'What does Kathy enjoy doing?' seemed to me at least as important a question as 'What are her medical problems?' Her joy in life and will to live kept her going through crises as much as any medication and treatment. Finding out what gave her pleasure was a discovery for all of us.

When Kathy was very young she did not seem to enjoy doing anything. Any change of activity or surroundings distressed her. We had to go out at times if only to go shopping or for hospital appointments. Over a period of time I found things she liked to do – going on the swings in the park, dabbling in a paddling pool and later splashing in a swimming pool, crawling and shuffling in a garden or park to explore, playing with small animals. I later realised that a lot of the problems we experienced with travelling were because she was uncomfortable. When she eventually got a wheelchair where she was comfortable and supported, she began to enjoy going for walks. We chose a wheelchair with the 12" pram wheels rather than the usual large wheeled self propelling models with castors in front. Kathy could not propel herself and the 12" wheels gave her a comfortable ride even over bumpy ground. We found she began to enjoy journeys by train or vehicle if she could travel in her wheelchair, rather than slide about uncomfortably on unsuitable seats.

TRAVELLING BY VEHICLE

I do not drive, so when I took Kathy on journeys I had to use public transport or taxis. I gave up trying to use buses and tube trains in London when Kathy was about seven years old, and I could no longer lift her up steep bus platforms or up and down the many stairs in tube stations. We could always use the London 'black' cabs fairly easily because Kathy's small wheelchair could be bumped up straight in the back; most cab drivers were very helpful. Travelling by taxi became less expensive when the former Greater London

Council introduced their taxi card scheme. It was a great day when Kathy got her first taxi card and could take a journey with her carers within a six mile radius for £1.00. When the GLC was abolished our London borough took on the scheme and Kathy continued to use the service. From the mid-1980s travelling became even easier with the new metro taxi cabs – the door opened out to a full right angle and a portable ramp was available, making it easier to wheel in even a full size wheelchair. Straps to secure the wheelchair made the journey safer. From 1991 financial problems meant that London boroughs cut back on the number of journeys members of the scheme could make each year.

During the 1980s many local authorities introduced a 'Dial a ride' scheme, whereby disabled people could register to use specially adapted vehicles for journeys. This service together with the taxi card scheme made it possible for disabled people who could not drive themselves to travel to visit friends or follow leisure pursuits at a reasonable cost.

We tried all sorts of arrangements for travelling as a family. We eventually used a Leyland Sherpa van, with side windows. A garage installed a fold-up ramp to the side door, and we wheeled Kathy up in her wheelchair, and then secured the chair with safety straps bolted through the floor. She was safe and comfortable and had a marvellous view as we drove. We used the van for camping, and had a wide bunk base in the back that could be used for changing Kathy's pads on long journeys. Journeys now became a real pleasure for Kathy; she loved driving at speed, looking out at passing traffic and scenery, and listening to her favourite music.

SWIMMING

Kathy always enjoyed her baths and we began to take her swimming, first to children's pools and then to the adult ones. It was good for her to be in the water, where her weight was supported. She was able to move her arthritic joints in a way she never could on dry land. At first we held her all the time; then we put armbands on arms and legs; then we found that if we put armbands just on her arms, she would make the effort to keep her head up and she began to try to move away from us deliberately, to explore moving and splashing in the water. Kathy never learned to swim; she laughed when she was enjoying herself and would swallow water, or a vigorous splash would take her head under. We tipped her up to empty the water out and waited until she had stopped coughing, and then she wanted to be off again. She had no fear, but we did have to stay close in case she swallowed too much water or her head went under more than momentarily.

We have tried swimming pools all over the country – council pools, open air pools, pools in hotels and leisure complexes. Until the 1980s there was no easy access or adapted changing facilities for disabled people. We might be offered a store room to change Kathy on the floor. I would have to hold her up against me in a public shower. We could hand Kathy down into the pool from one to the other because she was small and light, but this was not so easy for our friends whose children were larger, or for disabled adults. Now, more pools have hoists to help people to get in. When councils began to adapt facilities we tried many different pools to find the best. The pools with the most comfortable and spacious adapted facilities were not necessarily the ones with the most welcoming staff. The warmest and most attractive pools did not always have the best facilities. I did take Kathy swimming by myself at times, but it was hard work and it meant I could not relax for a moment. When I went with her father or a friend we often found facilities very cramped.

Carers may worry that a disabled person may be incontinent in the pool. This happens anyway with babies and young children. Pools are treated to kill infections and the water should be regularly checked for organisms. Nevertheless one would not want to add to the possibility of a health problem. With some people with multiple disabilities it is simply a question of communication, of enabling them to use the toilet or a pad immediately before going in the pool, and being ready to take them out when they indicate they need to go again. With people like Kathy there are not always such clear indications. Although Kathy was doubly incontinent, there was some evidence that she was able to make some effort for a period of time as she got older. We judged the situation according to how she was. If when we changed her into her swimming costume we found she had recently had a bowel movement and passed urine, we cleaned her carefully and just put her into her costume, watching carefully in the pool for any signs that we should take her out because she needed to go again. At other times we would put a pad inside tightly fitting plastic pants, and put her costume on over. A highly absorbent sanitary towel would be adequate for many people for a relatively short period. We did find that we needed the private adapted facilities afterwards because she needed a thorough shower to get rid of the chlorine, and would need her pad on immediately.

We met variable reactions from other swimmers. Kathy liked the children's pool because she loved to watch the babies and toddlers. Children are very direct and would come up to us in the water and stare, and say things like, 'What happened?' We would explain about Kathy's disabilities; if children just stared or made remarks, we would speak to them and tell them about Kathy, introducing her to them and asking their names. We took Kathy in the adult pool for periods because she liked the feel of splashing in the deep water, but we did have to establish a safe corner and watch out for fast swimmers.

Most people with multiple disabilities get cold very easily. We often started Kathy off in the children's pool where it was warmer, gave her a session in the big pool and then brought her back to the children's pool to warm her up. Some pools run sessions for disabled people and heat the pool to a higher temperature for those periods. A hot shower afterwards, a vigorous rub dry with a big towel and quick dressing with warm clothes make shivering and colds less likely.

We found that even if Kathy was not too well or had previously had fits, we would take her all the same and see how she was when we got there. Sometimes we turned round and went home if she had more fits or was very drowsy, but often she livened up when she heard the sounds of the pool. We took small objects such as table tennis balls and bath toys as well as larger plastic balls for her to play with, and she would stretch to get and throw them in a way she was less likely to do on dry land. Apart from the physical benefits of exercise in the water, we usually noticed that Kathy was more animated and cheerful afterwards, stimulated by the experience and the company, even if she was tired.

THEATRES, CINEMAS AND CONCERTS

I did take Kathy to these places when she was younger, but soon gave up. Access was not always easy, and it was difficult to make her comfortable. She got impatient waiting for the performance to start, and if she was enjoying herself she made happy sounds. At a West End Theatre where we had gone as a family to see 'Winnie the Pooh' I was asked to take Kathy out as she was making sounds, and she and I spent the whole performance in the bar.

We did take her to street festivals and open air performances, and she enjoyed these. She particularly enjoyed morris dancing, and some of the street theatre and festivals in France. It did not matter so much in these circumstances if she made a noise, and sometimes it was positively encouraged. I also noticed that as she got older she did get slightly more patient while waiting for a performance to start.

We began to try again. We went to several performances at a local music hall which had re-opened, offering a wide variety of shows – plays, pantomimes, musicals, folk groups from abroad. Kathy loved Russian music so we first tried the Georgian Folk Ensemble. There was easy access for the wheelchair into the theatre but not thereafter to the main seating area. The person in the wheelchair and those with them had to stay in the bar area, sitting at a table. This had its advantages, although we had to position Kathy carefully to make sure she had a good view. If she got impatient we could wheel her back, or take her out. We could bring some favourite foods, which usefully filled the gap between it all going quiet and something actually happening. She recognised many of the tunes on this first occasion as she had the tapes at home, and she loved the bright costumes and dancing. It was a great success, and we and other carers regularly took her after that. We found we could make successful trips to some other local venues; often success depended as much on the attitude of those running the theatre as on the physical access.

We also took her up to the National Theatre to their foyer performances. These were free and took place in the area by the bars and coffee bar. You could come and go as you pleased. We saw steel bands, folk groups, dancers and classical music performances. Kathy felt less restricted in the informal atmosphere and watched and listened intently.

Her friend, Victoria, who has a very similar level of disability, has gone with carers to the Festival Hall, the Barbican and other concert venues. There have been problems, and her carers have been asked to take her out at times when she expresses herself very loudly. They have found that taking carefully chosen snacks can help. Victoria's carers have engaged staff in discussions to establish her right to attend concerts, and consider the best ways of allowing her to do this without interfering with the pleasure of others. It is useful, for instance, for her to be able to sit near an exit so she can be taken out quickly if she needs to be. There are disabled people without learning difficulties who nevertheless make involuntary sounds as a result of some aspect of their disability. Long campaigning has resulted in better physical access for disabled people to concerts and theatres, although there is still a long way to go. It is just as important once they are there that problems such as those outlined above are dealt with. If it is felt important enough, a solution can be found.

GOING OUT FOR THE DAY

We go out to enjoy ourselves. It needed more effort to organise an outing with Kathy, but it was worth it; if she enjoyed herself, we were more likely to. We went out as a family, with friends, with small groups and on large outings. Groups like Kith and Kids, a voluntary organisation for people with disabilities, their families and carers, are good for encouraging everyone to go out into the usual places, regardless of hang-ups about what might be considered unusual physical appearance or inappropriate behaviour. Sometimes you need the support of other parents and carers to develop the courage to use public places.

A group of us, parents and care staff took our children out for the day to Knebworth House. We borrowed a council bus and loaded everyone up, the wheelchairs, the food, and the pads and other supplies. It was pouring with rain all the way there and when we arrived. We ate lunch in the bus; the adults all had a glass of wine to keep their spirits up. We were all very cheerful when we went to the cafeteria for a hot drink. It was very full. Two of us took our children in their wheelchairs to the only available space; within minutes the long table had emptied. The rest of the group joined us and we were able to be good humoured about the attitudes we encountered because we had our solidarity as a group. It is only fair to say that you do not always meet prejudice or indifference, and often members of the public are genuinely interested and helpful. People just need to be themselves, look at disabled people without staring, speak to them directly if they want to and only to a carer if they get no reply, accept that unusual behaviour may occur as a result of the disability. We enjoyed the rest of our day together, despite the rain and the fits three of the children had on the miniature railway. We sang on the journey back, the children were tired but happy, and we all agreed it had been worth it.

When Kathy was much younger I appreciated the efforts of friends to include us in their outings. It was more trouble for them because we had to carry large amounts of supplies, and look for places where I could change Kathy's pads. In cafes and restaurants and on beaches Kathy might make a noise or draw attention or remarks. Without these experiences Kathy would not have gradually learned to be more relaxed and to enjoy herself, and I would not have gained the confidence to take her on such outings by myself.

Our day trips with Kathy included visits to fairs, stately homes, festivals, the country and the seaside. We sometimes went by coach or train, but usually travelled in our own van. We took plenty of pads, wipes and damp facecloths in plastic bags; sets of clean clothes; a plastic sheet and a blanket, for sitting out and also for changing her. We always took her medication lists and plenty of supplies of medication. It was important to carry supplies of any specialist equipment, in Kathy's case naso-gastric tubes and syringes. Once we had experienced a vehicle breakdown, we made sure we carried blankets and pillows in case of a long wait. As Kathy got older we were more likely to eat out on a day trip, but she continued to enjoy picnics and we usually took food and drink in case of breakdown. I saved up old bottles and jars and made up dosages of medication ready to give, so we could just put the used containers in a rubbish bin. We got skilful at finding quiet corners to change her. We became accustomed to dealing with fits and other problems; it was usually more a case of reassuring anxious members of the public. In later years we might need to change Kathy's naso-gastric tube while we were out for the day, perhaps in the grounds of a stately home or on a beach.

As well as all the usual day trips, we found Kathy enjoyed visits to large shopping centres such as Milton Keynes, big markets and superstores. She also got much pleasure from being walked along the banks of canals and rivers, as well as taking boat trips. She was always more of a city person, but as she got older she seemed to appreciate country scenery more, especially if it was spectacular, such as mountains or river gorges. We noticed she liked walking in woods and forests and expressed her pleasure very audibly. We thought this was because of the changing light and shadow patterns, which she obviously enjoyed.

It seemed that, as Kathy could only move herself very short distances on the floor, she really appreciated being able to be moved about in her wheelchair or on transport. On days when we were busy in the house and she began to think we were not going out even for a short walk, she began to complain and look for her jacket to lean towards and give us the hint.

HOLIDAYS

When Kathy was very small, holidays meant going to stay with my parents or friends. I worried about her wetting and soiling beds and furniture; I watched anxiously for damp patches on furniture and carpets as she crawled about; I mopped up her dribble constantly. The experience of going away and the change of surroundings was good for all of us. Without the experiences Kathy would never have gradually accepted changes; if I had not given it a try, I would not have got better at managing the practical side.

Our first holiday on our own was an experience. Kathy's brother had been very ill following two mastoid operations. The doctors thought a change of air would do him good. I booked the three of us into a boarding house in Hastings for a fortnight. Peter was five and Kathy was three. Mercifully, Kathy slept for much of the journey. The first night Kathy screamed constantly; we all ended up in one bed. Next day I tried to keep her awake all day. The same thing happened at night. After the third night I took her to a local GP. She was still screaming at 9.00 a.m. and we were ushered through a crowded surgery after five minutes to see the doctor. I explained that Kathy was often like this at home but she seemed to be much worse since we had come away. I had not accepted medication to make her sleep before now, but the doctor suggested I try it for the holiday period. I used it and at least we all got a few hours sleep, and so did the rest of the guests. The weather was lovely and we did enjoy ourselves, on the beach, walking and going further afield on coach trips. We had to eat out at times and sometimes it went well, sometimes it was a disaster with food and crockery on the floor. The holiday certainly did Peter good, and I gained confidence in managing things.

We also went on some wonderful holidays with Kith and Kids to Churchtown Farm, a field study centre run by the Spastics Society in Cornwall. I usually chose to go by train with Kathy, as it gave more freedom of movement. On one occasion I travelled down with my friend Jean, whose daughter Victoria had a similar level of disability to Kathy. Victoria had not had as much experience of travelling. We were sitting in a first class compartment with seats removed to accommodate the wheelchairs. Victoria became very unhappy and loudly complained. I had long ago discovered how calming music was to Kathy in these circumstances. I took her earphones off, and we turned the volume of the Mozart on the tape recorder up so that we could all enjoy it. Gradually Victoria's howls subsided and she became calm. We gave the girls their food and opened a bottle of wine for ourselves. Then we realised that the carriage had emptied, and we had it all to ourselves.

At Churchtown Farm we went out every day, whatever the weather. Everyone took part in the activities, whether it meant volunteers hauling a wheelchair up a hill or through a river, or carrying it up the stairs of a stately home. Kathy went on a boat, helped to set food traps for small mammals and handle them before releasing them into the wild, explored beaches and rock pools and went on every variety of walk. When we got back after one holiday I realised the wheelchair was very creaky. When we went to have it checked, they asked us where on earth it had been. I then recalled that Kathy had gone in it through rivers and onto the seashore, right into the water so that she could experience the waves and see the sea creatures and seaweed.

As a family we began to rent cottages for a week or a fortnight's holiday, trying different parts of the country. We needed our big van for the supplies. We found that Kathy began to enjoy going to a different house, examining the arrangements with a particular interest in the kitchen. In some of the smaller cottages the bedrooms were tiny and cosy; once she slept in a box bed. This sort of holiday gave us the freedom to plan the day according to how Kathy was, to cook the sort of meals she liked and to deal with the mess and washing privately. Sometimes we managed to rent a cottage which had the use of a swimming pool, and we noticed how much she benefited from daily dips in the water. Sometimes Kathy was ill while we were away. Our Community Health Council would find out for us the name and address of the hospital nearest to where we were staying, in case of problems. Sometimes we had to use this information, or go to the local doctor. In these circumstances it was very useful to have the care book and medication details with us to provide all the relevant information.

Holidays with Kathy were more of a change than a rest. We used to go away without her at times, often to France. After one very pleasant holiday there we thought we would like to try taking Kathy to France. She liked hot weather – it seemed to ease her arthritic joints. She was more relaxed about changes as she was getting older, and we thought the stimulation of the journey and the different atmosphere of a foreign country would do her good.

The first time we travelled by ferry on the Newhaven–Dieppe route. This turned out not to be the best arrangement. The journey was four hours, long enough to be quite tiring but not long enough for any of us to settle down for a proper rest. We investigated a ferry company which did a longer, overnight crossing the next year, booked up a holiday home and travelled from Portsmouth to St Malo in Brittany. Some ferry companies do inclusive packages with gites (holiday homes) to rent and ferry crossings, and the brochures give details of accommodation suitable for people with disabilities. We booked cabins and notified the company in advance of Kathy's need for disabled access and facilities.

On arrival at the terminal you tell the people who book you in, and they organise you on to the ship so that your vehicle is next to the lift. Kathy enjoyed the excitement of the embarkation on the ferry; the first time we drove up the ramp of the ship into the hold she gave a great shout of delight. Kathy would be carried up by a large crew member. We left her wheelchair in our vehicle as she was relatively small and did not use it in the cabin, but it is possible to go up in the lift in the wheelchair. There is not full wheelchair access to the whole of the ship, but there are cabins which are fully accessible and have appropriate facilities. We would either take food on board or, depending on the hour, carry her to the restaurant. The crew did offer to bring a meal to the cabin if we wanted it.

Kathy was on very complex medication by this stage in her life, and she had bowel disease causing severe and frequent diarrhoea. I made up a bag with medication and pre-measured doses in clean old bottles. We had a handy tablet crusher and took small bottles of mineral water to use. Sometimes we had to give the medication in the ferry queue, depending on the time. I packed up carrier bags with complete changes of old clothes I had saved, pads, plastic bags and cleaning materials. I included plenty of bed pads to put on the bunk. Whenever Kathy had a disaster I cleaned and changed her, and then tied all the discarded old clothes and pads into plastic bags for later collection. I made sure I always had spare naso-gastric tubes on the ferry and lots of syringes for giving her medication.

Kathy liked the bunks in the cabins, especially on one ship where there were little curtains to draw, which fascinated her. She settled to sleep once the lights were out, and always slept soundly. The morning routine was busy, cleaning and changing her and giving medication. A crew member goes round giving an early morning call. While I drank strong black coffee I would give Kathy her breakfast, prepared at home the day before and carried in a glass jar. The stewards like to clear the cabins early on; we would sit with Kathy with the cabin door open, until we got the signal to go to the car deck. You need to check the night before what the exact arrangements are for escorting you to the car deck as they vary according to which ship you are on.

After an early start Kathy would often sleep for the next two or three hours, giving us a good start on our journey. We continued the old clothes system on our journey out, dumping any soiled items in plastic bags rather than carry dirty washing to the holiday place. We travelled in this way with Kathy to the Limousin, the Auvergne and several times to Brittany. She especially enjoyed the warmer areas, and was stimulated by the different language, food and atmosphere. It is possible to book a holiday home very near one of the ferry ports so that not much driving is involved. We stayed close to St Malo in Brittany more than once, and found plenty to do in the town and nearby resorts. Kathy particularly enjoyed the short boat trip across the bay to Dinard, where there is a coastal path with good access for wheelchairs.

We always made the following arrangements:

1. We took two full sets of medication supplies, each with more than enough for the length of the holiday. On arrival we kept one set in the holiday home and one in our vehicle. We made sure we had ample spares of any specialist items – in Kathy's case naso-gastric tubes, syringes, rectal valium for fits and Dioralyte sachets in case of severe diarrhoea. We kept Kathy's medication all together in a large plastic box with medicine pots, tablet crusher and a small bottle of mineral water.

2. We were sometimes able to get the name of a professional colleague of one of Kathy's doctors and a recommended nearby hospital in case of

emergency. If not, we found out on arrival where the nearest hospital was situated, and the local doctor; the local tourist information centre will give you this information.

3. We carried a letter from Kathy's doctor outlining her condition and listing the medication she took. If special equipment is required, especially if you need to carry needles, it is probably helpful for this to be mentioned.

4. At one time you had to take special holiday insurance out for a person with disabilities; the usual holiday insurance was not valid. In recent years we found that most holiday companies accepted the disabled person on the usual insurance, provided the doctor wrote a letter stating that the disabled person (or, as the insurance company say, someone with a pre-existing medical condition) was not travelling against doctor's advice. You need to check this by specifically asking the insurance company at the time of booking the holiday, and checking the wording of the letter they require. Unless you double check in this way that the disabled person is covered by the insurance, you could be in a situation where they possibly had an accident totally unconnected with their disability such as breaking a leg or an injury from something falling on them, and you would then not be covered for medical treatment and special arrangements for the journey home.

It makes sense to try and combine both this letter and the letter referred to in point number 3 – an example is given below:

Doctor's Name,
Address.
Telephone Number.
Date.

To whom it may concern

Katherine Sirockin, d.o.b. 17.11.63, suffers from cerebral palsy, rheumatoid arthritis, grand mal epilepsy and collagenous colitis.

I am aware of the arrangements for her holiday abroad and I would confirm that she is not travelling against medical advice.

Her medication is as follows:

Epilim syrup	500mg, 500mg, 700mg
Tegretol susp.	200mg, 200mg, 200mg
Ketovite Liquid	5ml
Ketovite Tablets	1 tablet, 1 tablet, 1 tablet
Soluble aspirin	600mg, 600mg, 600mg
Prednisol	10mg, 5mg
Azathioprine	25mg, 25mg
Clobazam	10 mg at night
Stesolid Valium	5 mg for rectal use in severe fitting

Katherine carries naso-gastric tubes size 10 fine gauge luer fitting and 20 ml syringes for giving medication through the tube.

In case of emergency, please contact me for further information at the telephone number above, or her hospital Consultant, Dr. ---, Telephone Number: ---.

Yours sincerely,

Dr. ------

Make sure that this letter is obtained and dated no earlier than about a month before you travel. If you go on holiday a second time, get a new letter written. If you can get the letter translated into the language of the country you are visiting this would be useful; carry the English copy as well.

5.   I took a complete set of protective pillow cases, sheets, draw sheets and duvet cover and replaced all the bedding on her bed at the place we would be staying with her own pillows and duvet. I saved old torn sheets for draw sheets which could then be thrown away after use.

We found when we first went to France that access for wheelchairs was not good. It is still true that in the narrow streets of old towns and villages it is not always easy to push a wheelchair, but other facilities such as parking and toilet facilities have improved a great deal. French people did not seem as accustomed to seeing disabled people out and about but we found most very willing to help. When we stopped at one restaurant for Sunday lunch, breaking a long journey and with Kathy very unwell, the people offered to bring her a couch. In another restaurant the waiter brought her little treats in between courses when he noticed she was not eating very well. We have very happy memories of a village festival with a huge barbecue and many country activities, where people came up and spoke to Kathy and introduced their children.

Kathy did sometimes have problems while we were abroad. Once her diarrhoea became much worse, with vomiting. Because by this time she was using a naso-gastric tube for drugs and fluids, we were able to prevent her from becoming dehydrated by giving her Dioralyte frequently; otherwise we would have had to seek medical help. On another occasion, she had a series of severe grand mal fits. We made the decision to stop as planned at an hotel, put her straight to bed and kept everything calm and quiet. She slept, but began fitting again the next morning. Again we took the decision to manage it ourselves and travel on to get the ferry as planned. You have to judge at the time whether the need for medical intervention is urgent, how much you can do by your usual management, and whether it is better to get back to familiar surroundings as soon as possible. We did decide after that episode that we would not in future plan any holiday in France that was more than one day's drive from the ferry, as such crises were more difficult to manage during very long journeys.

On one holiday we could not get our usual overnight crossing, so we had to take a long day crossing and book into an hotel on arrival. This was a new venture. I packed a whole suitcase for Kathy – several pairs of old pyjamas, a set of ancient tattered bed linen, protective covers for mattress, pillows, duvet, favourite dolls and toys, medication in ready prepared dosages, ready-prepared breakfast, portable electric kettle, soya milk powder, jug and fork for mixing, pads and wipes, plastic bags, music cassettes and player, lots of plastic bags. Kathy settled very well. In the morning we bathed her, gave her medication and breakfast, and took our huge sealed bag of rubbish out. She was then settled and calm enough to come into breakfast with us. We now felt confident enough to stay for longer periods in hotels both in the UK and in France – and no cooking or washing up! Kathy rose to the occasion and enjoyed eating in the hotel restaurant. If the hotel had a pool, this was an added bonus. Kathy enjoyed the routine of getting up slowly, going out for a half or whole day, maybe picnicking, coming back and playing on the floor, maybe going for a swim, and then having dinner in the restaurant.

One of our last happy memories is of a week's holiday in Normandy in a hotel, a few weeks before Kathy died. She was often not well but if we organised rest periods, she could cope with and enjoy going out, and she loved the evening meal ritual in the restaurant. On our last day we took her well wrapped up on a windy walk round Cap la Hogue and then for a meal in a smart restaurant.

It is sensible to check with a hotel beforehand about access to rooms and facilities. We would express a preference for a bath for Kathy, for instance, because of her particular needs. We had to sleep in the same room because she might need attention during the night; in many hotels this meant simply putting a single bed in the room in addition to ours. Ask about special diets and check when the food comes to the table. We took Kathy's dairy-free margarine and soya milk and these would be stored in the hotel fridge, and brought to the table when required.

PUBS

When Kathy was still very impatient waiting for food and drink, sitting outside in a pub garden was often more bearable. As she got older she positively enjoyed the atmosphere and we and other carers often took her to pubs, especially where there was live music. Kathy was physically small and appeared much younger than her actual age, so there were times when we were questioned; we began to think of carrying a birth certificate to show!

CLUBS

There are specialised clubs for people with disabilities, and these can provide access to many activities and company. Increasingly, people with disabilities want to feel they have access to the same facilities as others. I think there may be room for both. It was an advantage, for example, to be able to go with Kathy to a swimming session exclusively for disabled people, which was less crowded, where the water was often deliberately warmer, and where there were extra helpers. We noticed how Kathy empathised with other people with disabilities and was interested for instance in other people's wheelchairs. It can be relaxing and supportive to meet at times with others who share and understand your difficulties. It is very difficult for children with severe multiple disabilities to join some of the usual children's organisations such as Cubs, Brownies and Woodcraft Folk. If the carers of the child really believe they want to and would benefit from joining, then they should go and insist on giving it a try. In the same way there will be adult clubs and organisations where the person with multiple disabilities may wish to participate. The key question must be to interpret the wishes and interests of the person with the disabilities accurately- then, be adventurous, and insist that those in charge in the organisation give it a try.

Kathy benefited for some years from attending a local sports evening for disabled people. She loved the swimming and enjoyed the company. She liked going to the cafe afterwards but she could not realistically take part in any of the other activities. She enjoyed being a spectator at some activities but not generally at sports, so we were guided by her wishes and limited her attendance to the parts of the evening she enjoyed.

FOOTBALL MATCHES, BANGER RACING, SPEEDWAY, THE DOGS, ETC

Try something different! Just as Kathy loved to be moved in her wheelchair or in a vehicle, as she could not move independently, so she enjoyed watching vehicles move at speed. We only occasionally took her to watch banger racing, but each time it was a resounding success. She loved the atmosphere, noise and excitement. There are often all sorts of physical difficulties in attending such events but it is worth taking some risks for new experiences. Again it is good for the disabled person to have the same access as others, to be in the crowd, but this has to be reconciled with getting a good view, safe evacuation if necessary, and being able to get into, say, a football ground without having the necessity to queue.

ADULT EDUCATION CLASSES

In the 1980s there were some remarkable developments in the provision of adult education classes for people with learning disabilities. There were still problems of access for people with physical disabilities, and transport was not easily provided for those who could not travel by themselves. Few of these classes were actually very suitable for people like Kathy. There is a strong case for the value of continuing education for people with multiple disabilities, as well as for pursuing hobby and leisure interests, but much more thought needs to go into how the classes are organised, and transport there remains a crucial issue. The development of communication skills and music appreciation would be two obvious subjects to offer.

I know of drama groups who work with an integrated approach, including people with disabilities in their productions and adapting their work to use people's strengths. It is so pleasant and exciting to take part in drama productions that this seems an obvious area to develop for the benefit of people with multiple disabilities. A friend organised a Christmas production in the residential unit for people with multiple disabilities where she worked. Every resident had at least one part, all dressed in costumes to reflect the Victorian theme, there was live music and audience participation. Some of the staff had not believed it would be possible – the pleasure and pride of both residents and their families in the audience proved them wrong.

WHOSE LEISURE?

Kathy shared many interests with us. Indeed we developed some interests from her exercise of preferences, notably our discovery of early music from her enthusiasm. In other cases, we did not always enjoy the same things. Although Kathy was not very keen on pop music in general, she did enjoy a disco with loud bass, the lights, the full works. She jigged on our laps or in her wheelchair, loved to be wheeled round fast in the strobe lights* and liked to 'dance' held against one of us as long as our arms would stand it. We put up with it at times because of her obvious enjoyment, but it was preferable if she did this activity with other young people and carers who were also enjoying themselves.

*If you care for someone with epilepsy, their fits may be triggered by strobe lights; this only affects a minority of people with epilepsy, but you need to be aware of the risk.

FURTHER INFORMATION

AA Guide for the Disabled, Automobile Association, PO Box 50, Basingstoke, Hants RG21 2EA. Tel: 0256–20123. A guide which lists hotel services and facilities, advisory bodies, motorway services, restaurants, etc.

Air Transport Users Committee, 2nd Floor, Kingsway House, 103 Kingsway, London WC2B 6XQ. Tel: 071–242–3882. Advice and information for disabled people travelling by air. Booklet 'Care in the Air'.

Break, 20 Hookshill Road, Sheringham, Norfolk NR26 8NL. Seaside holiday centres for children and adults with profound disabilities.

Camping for the Disabled, 20 Burton Close, Dawley, Telford, Shropshire, TF4 2BX. Tel: 0743–61889. Information and advice on camping in Britain and Europe.

Discos for Handicapped Children, Toc H, 1, Forest Close, Wendover, Aylesbury, Bucks. Tel: 0296–62 39 11.

Equal Play, 30 Powell Road, London E5 8DJ. Tel: 081–985–7407. Information on toys, leisure, holidays, etc. for handicapped children.

Ferry Services: You can get up to date information from your local travel agent or from the A.A. Ferry Guide, address above. Make a list of the facilities you need and check that the company can provide them before you book.

Gateway Clubs, National Federation of, 117/123 Golden Lane, London EC1Y ORT. Tel: 071–454–0454. Runs clubs in all areas for people with learning disabilities, some for younger children.

Handicapped Adventure Playground Association, Fulham Palace, Bishops Avenue, London SW9 6EA. Tel: 071–731–1435. Information about toys and play; advice on setting up adventure playgrounds for handicapped children.

Kith and Kids, The Irish Centre, Pretoria Road, Tottenham, London N17 8DX. Tel: 081–801–7432.

Leisure Resource Pack; edited by Loretto Lambe; written by James Hogg. Developed by MENCAP PRMH Project. Published by MENCAP 1991.

MENCAP Holiday Services, 119 Drake Street, Rochdale, Lancs OL16 1PZ. Tel: 0706–54111. Holiday homes and schemes. Holiday accommodation list of self catering, camping/caravan, hotel addresses.

National Trust, 42 Queen Anne's Gate, London SW1H 9AS. Tel: 071–222–9251. Produces guide: 'Facilities for the disabled.'

One to One, 404 Camden Road, London N7 OSJ. Tel: 071–700–5574. Befriending scheme encouraging people with disabilities to join in community and leisure activities.

Outdoor Activity Centres, The Sports Council, 16 Upper Woburn Place, London WC1H 0QP. Tel: 071–388–1277.

Railcard for Disabled People, British Rail, Dept. XX, PO Box 28, York, YO1 1FB. Produces a leaflet 'British Rail and Disabled Travellers'.

RADAR, 12 City Forum, 250 City Road, London EC1V 8AF. Tel: 071–637–5400. Excellent range of guides and directories covering leisure, sports, outdoor activities, holidays and transport.

Scottish Tourist Board, 2 Ravelston Terrace, Edinburgh, EH4 3EU. Tel: 031–332–2433. Information on facilities in Scotland for disabled people.

Spastics Society, 12 Park Crescent, London W1N 4EQ. Tel: 071–636–5020. Information sheets on holiday services for people with cerebral palsy. Runs several holiday homes.

Sports Centres for Disabled People, RADAR, address above. A guide to centres in England and Wales.

Swimming for Disabled People, 3 Knoll Crescent, Northwood, Middlesex. HA6 1HH. Tel: 0923–827142.

Toilet Key Scheme for Disabled People. Contact RADAR for details, address above.

Transport, Department of, 2 Marsham Street, London SW1P 3EB. Produce 'Door to Door – a guide to transport for people with disabilities' with details of facilities for disabled people for all forms of transport, including sea and air. Free to voluntary organisations; can be bought from HMSO.

Welsh Tourist Board, Brunel House, 2 Fitzalan Road, Cardiff CF2 1UY. Tel: 0222–49 99 09. Information for disabled visitors.

For Many Other References and Details of Particular Holiday Homes and Centres, SEE: *Useful Addresses for Special Needs* by Ann Worthington, 10 Norman Road, Sale, Cheshire M33 3DF. Tel: 061–905–2440.

CHAPTER 21

FAMILIES AND FRIENDS

Friends who have disabled children understand and can cope with the often messy and disruptive consequences of social activities. Families have to learn. This can be difficult if they are also finding it painful to accept that the cousin, nephew, grandchild or whoever has a severe disability. It depends on what is important. It is sensible for carers to take precautions to avoid obvious mess; I took large bed pads to put on settees and a mat for the floor. I took my kits in plastic bags for cleaning Kathy up. I made sure she always had bibs when visiting and I mopped her dribble if possible before it got on to carpets and furniture. I could not guarantee that she would not grizzle or even scream for hours on end. I had to be watchful for her grabbing ornaments, utensils, other people's food and drink, or doing her favourite tablecloth trick of clearing the table at one go.

If the fear of mess, noise and disruption takes away the enjoyment of the visit, there is no point in continuing. If family members want to build a relationship with the child who has profound intellectual and multiple disabilities, they must see them regularly and engage in activities to get to know them. Other children can gain sensitivity and insight by relating to and playing with a friend or family member who has severe disabilities; they will gain pleasure by giving pleasure. Kathy showed obvious happiness when she met her cousins, or children of friends, and they were able to see her as a real person, not a nuisance or a curiosity. One of her cousins said to me after she had died, 'Kathy knew she was older than us – you could just tell'. He felt this strongly, even though in her twenties Kathy still played with toys and appeared physically to be a young child.

Try visits on home ground, where at least parents and carers are organised to mop and clean up. Go out on picnics and trips together, where there is no need to worry about making a mess. Be honest with family members about the nature and extent of the disability. Do not allow people to pretend it is something maybe more acceptable, or less severe, for instance by telling other children that the disabled person is much younger than they actually are.

CELEBRATIONS

'What have we got to celebrate?' may be an honest if concealed reaction by parents of a child with severe disabilities. Each birthday brings reminders of what you would usually expect them to be doing at that age. Some birthdays, such as the eighteenth, are especially significant, as they usually mark the formal beginning of adulthood and independence.

We always celebrated Kathy's birthdays. Sometimes it was a small family affair. At other times we liked to include her wider family, her many friends and their families and carers. Giving and receiving gifts was important. People took obvious pleasure in choosing special things for Kathy. She often seemed to prefer the wrapping paper, but later, when no one seemed to be looking, she would creep over and examine her present. Sometimes she would react immediately and joyfully to a welcome gift, resulting in enormous pleasure for the giver.

Christmas and other special times were important. Kathy enjoyed rituals like decorating the tree, and seemed to begin to make some sense of the changes in the year marked by different occasions. Things that she seemed not even to notice in her early years had gradually been absorbed. Visits at such times to friends and members of the family, as well as giving pleasure, helped her to see similar celebrations in other settings.

Kathy enjoyed being involved in other people's celebrations too. She usually thought presents were for her, but gradually got the idea of giving as well as receiving, although she was always reluctant to let go of the parcel.

One problem was that Kathy always associated arriving at someone's home with having a meal. Her grandma had this all organised, with food timed to go on the table as we rang the bell. It was more difficult with people we knew less well, and a strategic sandwich came in useful to plug the gap.

MAKING IT WORK

Even those close to you may feel uneasy and anxious at being asked to relate to someone with profound intellectual and multiple disabilities. You must take the initiative, say what needs to be done, tell people when they get it right as well as when they make mistakes. If the occasion is an utter disaster, go home, try to see the funny side, and try again. You may be able to work out the reasons why it all went wrong; you may never know. You will learn quickly which of your old friends will stay friends; you will make new ones too. Your family will cope if they want to; you cannot worry about those who, for one reason or another, do not cope – it is their loss to miss the rewards of making a real effort to know and love someone who at first challenges all their expectations.

ILLNESS AND DEATH

If someone important to the disabled person you care for is very ill or dies, it is essential to help them to understand what is happening and to be involved. They should visit anyone who is ill and be involved in arrangements, including funerals when someone dies. It is not possible to know how much they will understand, but you can explain and involve them. It will be more frightening and bewildering if someone they love seems to disappear out of their lives. If another family is involved you will have to respect their feelings, but you can try and explain what you think should happen.

YOUR PARTNER

Your relationship with your partner will be subject to extra stresses, over and above the ones all marriages and relationships experience. Relationships are tested to the limit, and do not always survive. If they do survive, they are stronger than others which have not been tested so severely. You need to talk honestly about all the difficulties and try to draw strength from each other, not blaming the other one for things beyond your control, or mistakes which will happen. It is easy to get trapped on the treadmill of constant caring. You and your partner need time to yourselves, to talk, to enjoy the things you like doing together, to laugh. You need to make time to conserve enough energy to maintain and enjoy your sexual relationship. If possible you need to be able to go away together occasionally, even if it is just a weekend break. This means organising respite or substitute care. You have to convince yourselves first that this is necessary, then insist it is provided, then learn to trust the substitute carers, so you do not spoil your break by constant anxiety. How badly and frequently you need this time together depends on your individual circumstances. But if it can help to prevent total exhaustion and frustration with life and each other, you will be more likely to preserve your relationship during the inevitable crises.

If your partner cannot cope, or the pressures cause constant conflict, you must get help – from friends, from organisations such as RELATE, from your GP, from other family members. Friends in similar situations will understand best, and you can be honest with them. Sometimes it does not work out and your best course is to separate. If you do, remember that someone with profound intellectual and multiple disabilities will find it even harder to understand the break-up, and will not be able to express their anxieties in the normal way.

SINGLE PARENTS

Whatever the reason you are coping on your own, you feel as if you are carrying the whole burden. You need respite care and other services even more than couples. But most of all you need friends. Join a group where you will meet other parents and carers; you may meet other single parents. Try your local MENCAP group, Contact a Family, Kith and Kids (details at the end of the chapter.) If you are not working, consider whether a job, possibly part-time, would give you companionship and other interests. You may need extra services for this to happen.

BROTHERS AND SISTERS

I know I was never able to divide my time fairly between Kathy and her brother. She always had to come first, and it must have been particularly hard for him to be dragged along when he was small to her hospital appointments, visits to casualty, emergency admissions and constant visits during her many stays in hospital. As he got older he could at least stay with friends on some of these occasions, but Kathy's needs still came first. He saw Kathy in pain and very ill at times, and must have experienced confusing and conflicting feelings.

We did try to make time for him alone with us, to take him on holiday without Kathy. But he had to live with our tiredness, anxiety and short temper, as well as his own worries. Talking helped, friends helped, but nothing could take away the fundamental problems.

It is helpful if brothers and sisters can talk to others in the same position. This can happen spontaneously during activities organised by groups such as Kith and Kids and Contact a Family. Perhaps the opportunity for this to happen should not be left to chance.

I was not aware of these problems in the early years. Caught up in the day to day turmoil, I needed friends to help me notice.

All this is not to underestimate the way in which having a brother or sister with profound intellectual and multiple disabilities can help to develop qualities of patience, tolerance and understanding. Kathy's brother wrote a piece at school when he was about twelve, which showed the positive side of their relationship:

> 'Food doesn't play a very important part in my life. I eat because I enjoy it and because if I didn't I would die. To my sister, food is the biggest thing in her life.
>
> My sister is mentally handicapped. She can't walk or talk. Some would say that if you are like that, there is no point in living, that you don't understand anything if you are like that. But my sister knows what it means when you start laying the table. Even is she's in a bad mood, she will sit up and have a little chuckle to herself. She knows what it means when you put the knives and forks out on the table. She will often crawl over to the table or look at you as if to say, 'Come on then, hurry it up.'
>
> Then, when you put her bib on she will laugh, and she will help you to put it on sometimes. When you put her up to the table she will look at the door, waiting for someone to come with the food, and if the food doesn't come quickly she will bang on the table and give you dirty looks.
>
> But what's best of all is the look she gives you when you bring the food in, and then give her the first spoonful. Her whole face will light up, and she will give you a big smile.
>
> Every now and again she will sit back and give a satisfied sigh, and laugh to herself, or lean forward and chuckle at you, or even let out a little burp, look a little ashamed, and then chuckle to herself.
>
> And when she's finished her food, she doesn't finish there. She looks expectantly at your plate, and then you just have to give her some of your own food.
>
> Why does she get so much enjoyment out of food? I think that food is about the only thing she'll definitely get, day after day. She has no way of knowing that something will happen to her, apart from that she'll get her food. She enjoys the exercise of eating, and the pleasure of being surrounded by people at the table.'

FURTHER INFORMATION

Contact A Family, 170 Tottenham Court Road, London W1P 0HA. Contact Helpline: 071–383–3555. Information about local groups of parents and carers.

Gingerbread (One parent families), 35, Wellington Street, London WC2E 7BN. Tel: 071–240–0953.

Kith and Kids, The Irish Centre, Pretoria Road, Tottenham, London N17. Tel: 081–801–7432.

MENCAP, 123, Golden Lane, London EC1Y 0RT. Tel: 071–454–0454. Information about local groups.

One Parent Families National Council for, 255 Kentish Town Road, London NW5 2LX. Tel: 071–267–1361.

Relate (formerly Marriage Guidance Council), Herbert Gray College, Little Church Street, Rugby, Warks CV21 3AP. Tel: 0788–573241.

Single Parents Scottish Council for, 44 Albany Street, Edinburgh EH1 3QR. Tel: 031–556–3899 or 39 Hope Street, Glasgow G2 6AE. Tel: 041–221–1681.

SIBS, Mrs. P. Fairbrother, 170 Queens Road, Wimbledon, London SW19 8LX, or contact MENCAP. Support and contact for anyone with a mentally handicapped brother or sister.

PUBLICATIONS

Am I Allowed to Cry? Maureen Oswin, Souvenir Press, Human Horizons Series (1991). ISBN: 0 285 65096 3. A study of bereavement amongst people with learning difficulties.

CHAPTER 22

THE FUTURE – WILLS, TRUSTS AND GUARDIANS

PLANNING AHEAD

When you are fully occupied with the care of a baby or young child with profound intellectual and multiple disabilities, you will rarely have time to think very far ahead. Simply getting through each day, and searching and fighting for all that the disabled person needs, is more than a full time job. Perhaps, as the child grows older, you might start to think of the future. Events in the family may stimulate such thinking – a serious illness of one of the partners, a breakdown in the marriage, the death of a friend who also had a disabled child, problems with other children.

When my first marriage broke down, I took out a life insurance policy for the benefit of my two children, and that was the extent of my planning. I had good friends and I assumed that they and my family would see the children were all right, if anything happened to me. A year or two later, following a visit to MENCAP to discuss my worries about Kathy's education, I joined the Trusteeship Scheme which would ensure she had a regular visitor to look after her interests in the event of my death. The details of this scheme, some of which have changed since I joined it, are given in the last section of this chapter.

It was Kathy's first long-term residential placement that made me really think about the future for her, if I should die. She was neglected and possibly ill-treated, and required months of hospital treatment after I took her away. I had married again by now, and Kathy's stepfather was as concerned as I was about what had happened. While we were looking at alternative residential placements, we realised that even the best needed constant visiting, encouragement of staff and monitoring of concerns to maintain standards. To think that Kathy might end up in the worst places we saw, without us to fight for her interests, was horrifying. We began to judge everything by the 'under a bus' approach. We asked whether education, care provision, comforts and extras, health input and above all love, concern and interest would continue to be of the best quality for Kathy if we should both die 'under a bus' tomorrow. Day-to-day work and planning, and Kathy's constant ill health, still took up much of our energy, so there was no grand plan. However, in our future work for her we had these issues in mind, and began to search for and seize opportunities to build security for her needs when the chance came.

I have divided the main issues up under separate headings. This makes it easier to consider the implications of taking or not taking action. These implications are fully discussed in Gerald Sanctuary's book *After I'm Gone; What will happen to my handicapped child?* (details at the end of the chapter). Although some of the detailed advice in this book is inevitably out of date due to changes in the law and in government policy, the issues of concern to parents remain the same, and the book is worth reading because it makes you confront those issues.

I have concentrated on information which will be relevant to those planning ahead on behalf of a person with profound intellectual and multiple disabilities, as some options will not be available or appropriate for people with this degree of disability.

FUTURE CARE PLANS

It is possible that you are quite satisfied with your present care arrangements. If the disabled person is of school age they will have day provision for the school terms, and may even be at residential school. You may be receiving adequate respite care provision, or even be coping fine without it. If the disabled person you care for has left school, you have probably run into the first of a number of unforeseen problems – they may now be offered day care for only part of the week, or not at all. They will almost certainly have grown bigger, and may have a condition which leads to further deterioration. You may find that you yourself have less energy and resilience, and need some space for your own interests and relaxation. Do what seems best for everybody while you can; but in the meantime, plan ahead.

Do not forget the chance in a million. Going on holiday abroad with my husband and Kathy's brother, the thought struck me on the aircraft during some turbulence, suppose we were to crash and all die, who would attend to Kathy's interests? It was one of the thoughts that prodded us into further action when we returned home.

There is a further central issue. What about the interests of the person with the disabilities? I think it is usually true that no one else will ever give the loving care and attention to detail that parents do. However, I learned from Kathy, as she grew older, that this was not the only thing that mattered. Despite the profound nature of her disabilities and her worsening health, she continued to grow as a person, to improve her capacity to develop and sustain relationships, and to broaden her interests. She did like to spend time with others and she needed the stimulation of other people her own age, with or without disabilities. We had to learn to let go, and accept that, while she appreciated her time at home with us, she needed her own space as a young woman away from her parents. Investigating and planning these options takes time and energy, and is best done while you are relatively young and capable.

If your child is already in residential care, you will want to know if this will continue once they become an adult. If not, you will need to investigate what comes next. If your child is receiving regular respite care, you will need to find out if the arrangements will continue once they reach adult age, and what the options are for full time residential care if it is needed. If your child is at a residential school, you will need to decide whether you will be able to take her home full or part time when she reaches school leaving age, and what the day provision might be. If you decide you cannot, you will need to start making plans, at least by the time she reaches the age of 14. Children with statements should have a full assessment of their future needs between the ages of 13 and 14, and you should make sure this includes an assessment of future residential needs.

If you are caring for an adult, you can ask for an assessment of care needs under the 1990 NHS and Community Care Act. There are more details in Chapter 11, Respite and Residential Services.

The options for residential care for people with profound intellectual and multiple disabilities are as follows:

1. Long stay hospitals

2. Local authority units

3. NHS units

4. Private or voluntary homes, units or nursing homes

5. Fostering or boarding out

6. Independent living schemes.

The chapter 'Respite and Residential Services' gives some ideas for finding and choosing a suitable place. Although it is government policy to phase out long-stay hospitals, some remain because no alternatives have been planned for some of the residents. Some long-stay hospitals were split up into 'small' units which may still consist of 200 residents. Some have been split up into 'core and cluster' units, with a 'core' unit for those with more severe disabilities. Many long-stay hospitals have been rightly criticised in the past for poor standards of care, and even neglect. If this is what you are offered, visit before you turn the offer down, and see and discuss what the facilities are. Ask if there is a parents' group or similar organisation; ask if there are parents of residents who would be willing to talk to you. The local Community Health Council should have information about the facilities and standards of care.

However, do not accept that, because the person you care for has profound intellectual and multiple disabilities, they automatically need hospital care. In recent years local and health authorities, as well as charitable organisations, have successfully set up small scale residential units within the community which take people with such disabilities. It was once considered that such units could only take the more able. Provided they have adequate staffing, good access for wheelchairs and appropriate physical facilities such as adapted bathrooms, there is no reason why they should not accept any degree of disability. Visit any of these in your locality. If there are none, visit some further afield, and come back with information to challenge the policy of your local authority. There is information on finding out about such places at the end of Chapter 11.

Under the 1990 National Health Service and Community Care Act, local authorities will continue to provide residential services for those who need them, but will also buy in appropriate services. They are supposed to design a 'care package' according to the particular needs of the individual. This could mean paying for a place in a private or voluntary unit. They could also pay for care to be brought to the disabled person, in their own home. If you agree to this, bear in mind that if you die or become incapable, and there is no other relative or partner to continue in the family home and supervise the arrangements, it is not certain that a person with profound intellectual and multiple disabilities will be able to remain there. You might want to consider an 'independent living scheme' involving 24-hour care in council or housing association accommodation; this will need advance planning (see Chapter 12.) If you choose this option you will need to have someone ready to oversee the arrangements – an advocate, who may be a relative or a friend, or someone appointed by a voluntary organisation. There is more about this in the last section of this chapter.

However reluctant you may be to consider these things, remind yourself of the possible outcome if you do not. At a time when the disabled person has to suffer the shock of bereavement, their trauma may be made worse by being suddenly removed from familiar surroundings to live in a place that you would not have chosen for them.

MAKING A WILL

It is always essential to make a will. Most of us are not so rich that we can leave a fortune sufficient to pay for private care for the rest of the disabled person's life. However, many people will own a house. Those who are tenants will have personal possessions and insurance policies. Most people have at least some modest savings. The sum total of most people's effects is usually far more than they realise. You may have other children, and want to make sure whatever you have to leave is shared out fairly, so there are no arguments or bad feeling. If you die without leaving any will, your assets and effects may be disposed of in a way you would not have wished.

It is always important to get legal advice when drawing up your will. It is absolutely essential when writing any will which involves a person with a learning disability. There are extra legal considerations and traps in the laws on state benefits. These will affect people with profound intellectual and multiple disabilities most of all. Laws and tax rules change over time, and what is quite valid one year may later be useless. See a solicitor to start with. Because this is a specialised area, ask if the MENCAP solicitor can recommend one. MENCAP issue an information pack with guidance on the law about leaving property and money to people with learning disabilities.

Do not begrudge the expense of going to a solicitor. If finding a fee is a real problem, try your local law centre or see if a local charity or one concerned with the disabled person's condition can help. It can be more expensive to the person you care for in the long run if you do it yourself; for reasons you may not even be aware of, they could be deprived of the benefits you had intended for them.

Making your Will

1. If you see a solicitor, they will discuss how you want your goods, money and any property dealt with. They will advise you how taxes might affect this. They will advise how best to organise things for the benefit of those named in the will, including any special arrangements for someone with profound intellectual and multiple disabilities. Show

them the MENCAP information pack. They will then sort out appropriate wording and get the will typed.

2. The will must be signed and witnessed correctly, and the solicitor will advise about this.

3. The signed will needs to be kept in a safe place. The solicitor will keep it for you, or it can be stored at your bank. You will have a copy to keep.

4. If you have possessions – jewellery, furniture, books, pictures, and so forth – that you want to go to particular people, make a list with a note of the names of those you intend to give them to; this can be kept with your will.

5. You will need to name someone as executor; this person will make the funeral arrangements and then dispose of the money, property and so forth, as laid down in the will. The executor can be a friend or family member, or the solicitor. You can name someone as executor even if you have left something to them in your will. If you decide to ask the bank to be executor, find out about the fees and expenses they will charge.

LEAVING MONEY IN TRUST

Why cannot you just leave money or property to your son or daughter with a learning disability?

If she has a profound learning disability, she will not be considered able to control her own finances. Someone else will have to do it for her. To avoid exploitation of someone in this situation, the Court of Protection would probably be involved. There is more about this in the next section.

Why cannot I leave my money or property to my other children or relatives? I can trust them to see that my disabled daughter continues to have comforts and treats, and is generally well provided for.

First, a local authority paying for someone in residential care may challenge a will that did not leave the disabled person any share; if they were successful, they would use the money to pay for care costs; more in the section below. Second, if regular payments are made, it may be considered that there is a 'secret trust' and entitlement to local authority accommodation and benefits may be affected as above. Third, any money or property you leave to someone belongs to them. If they were to die, or perhaps divorce, others would have claims on the money and may not carry out the obligations to the disabled person.

So, how can I make sure that any money I leave for the benefit of my daughter with disabilities is actually used for extras and treats for her?

You should get advice on setting up a trust for her, which will come into force when both parents die, and will last while she lives. You name people to act as trustees – they can be relatives, friends or someone like a solicitor. They take charge of any money left to the trust and invest it as you have laid down. They are then responsible for making payments to your daughter to provide the extras you want her to enjoy. Remember:

1. There are different kinds of trust and you will need advice from a solicitor on what is best for your circumstances.

2. There are tax advantages and disadvantages according to the type of trust, and your particular financial circumstances. The solicitor will discuss this and advise you accordingly.

3. If your daughter is in residential care or likely to be after your death, it is still possible to set up a trust for providing her with extras, without the danger of the money being taken to pay towards residential fees, or leading to loss of state benefits. You will need to discuss with the solicitor the best form of trust for this purpose, and consider carefully the amount of money you want to set aside. Your solicitor will find it helpful to consult the MENCAP information pack to check details.

We will leave a substantial amount on our deaths, but not enough to pay entirely for private care for our daughter. Is there any way the money could be used to give her a better standard of care?

Under the 1990 NHS and Community Care Act trustees could use sums of money to top up residential costs if the local authority would otherwise not agree to a more expensive placement, which was nevertheless felt to offer a more appropriate level of care for your daughter.

MENCAP offers various services as follows:

1. The National Trustees for the Mentally Handicapped Limited manage individual trust funds for people with a learning disability. You need to contact them to see if the arrangements are suitable for your particular circumstances.

2. You can leave a sum of money to a charitable trust, such as the MENCAP Adcare Foundation. This gets round the problem of the private trust, as the money donated is used for the benefit of a large number of people with learning disabilities, not just your son or daughter. Because of the terms of the charitable status, you cannot expect your son or daughter to receive any specific amount or benefit from the money you leave. However, you can register a person with the Foundation as someone who may receive benefit in future. You then leave with your will a list of things that would be of benefit to the disabled person, for example. regular outings, replacing favourite items. You include a list of people who can discuss with the Foundation possible benefits to that person – perhaps a brother or sister, an uncle or aunt, a close friend, another parent.

3. Some parents leave their home to the MENCAP Homes Foundation; this or the proceeds of selling it can then be used to provide accommodation for a number of people with learning disabilities, including possibly their own son or daughter. The arrangements vary from area to area, but because staffing costs have to be raised in addition, this arrangement is not usually suitable for those with profound intellectual and multiple disabilities. You can find out more by contacting the Homes Foundation at the MENCAP address.

The arrangements you make will depend on your personal circumstances. The important thing is to get legal advice, and to make sure that any of the above arrangements or any others you make, are properly set out in a will. If you have relatives, grandparents perhaps, who may intend to leave money or property to the person with the disabilities, do talk to them about these matters; it would be a pity for their generosity to fail to benefit the person they loved.

Do make sure you check every few years that your will takes account of changes in the law, tax and government policy. Your solicitor will be able to advise if any changes need to be made.

THE COURT OF PROTECTION

It is better if someone with profound intellectual and multiple disabilities does not inherit sums of money or property directly. However, sometimes they do because of the will of a relative who does not understand the problems; or someone may die without leaving a will, and the disabled person may inherit a share. The Court of Protection manages property for people who cannot do it themselves. If you are administering a will like this, the solicitor will probably advise you apply to the Court of Protection for a Receiver to be appointed, who can be a relative or friend. The Receiver is then responsible for managing any property or money under the supervision of the Court. This will be the only way of managing things once money or property has come directly into the possession of someone with profound intellectual and multiple disabilities. Indeed, it will be necessary to ensure that the disabled person benefits from their inheritance, and not someone else. However, there are disadvantages:

1. Any money or money arising from the sale of property will be taken into account for Income Support benefit purposes, and benefit will be reduced or even lost according to the amount inherited. A local authority providing residential accommodation will also be able to have access to this money to pay charges.

2. Fees are payable each year to the Court of Protection.

3. The Receiver will need to seek approval for spending money and will need to present annual accounts, as well as managing any property or investments, arranging insurance, sales, etc. This could involve a great deal of work.

4. The procedures of the Court such as applying, getting approval for spending, etc. can be very slow.

For all these reasons, especially the first, it is better to try and avoid these matters ever coming to the Court of Protection. It is vital to make a will, and to get reliable advice about how money and property can be best managed, by trusts or some other method. This applies to parents, relatives, friends or anyone likely to want to leave something to a person with profound intellectual and multiple disabilities.

WHO WILL CARE LIKE ME?

It is unlikely that anyone can replace the parent or similar long-term carer. Parents may feel they do not want to place obligations on brothers or sisters, or other relatives. They hope they will continue to visit and take an interest, but do not feel they can expect them to take on the full burden of care and responsibility. If they want to, and this seems realistic, it can be considered; but remember, they may also become ill, suffer an accident or die – then the same problems will arise that have been discussed all through this chapter. Personal circumstances vary, so one or more of the following suggestions may be useful:

1. While your child is under 18 you can appoint a guardian in your will. A couple should do this in case they both die in an accident. Separated or divorced couples can each appoint a guardian. We named my husband as guardian in the event of my death, as he had not formally adopted the children from my previous marriage. Becoming guardian for a child with profound intellectual and multiple disabilities is a heavy responsibility. We made an agreement with friends who had a daughter similar to Kathy; in the event of either set of couples dying, the others would assume guardianship. We felt we understood what would be involved because of our similar experiences. We expected relatives to continue to take an interest, but we did not expect them to shoulder the whole burden. The arrangement also applied when either set of couples was on holiday abroad.

2. At present you cannot make guardianship arrangements for adults with profound intellectual and multiple disabilities. Remember also that parents of someone with learning disabilities over the age of 18 are not her legal guardians. Our solicitor helped us to frame a wording that expressed our wish for our friends to continue to act as if they were Kathy's guardians after she was 18. He felt that in practice in most situations this would be accepted, for instance in giving information to care staff in residential units, discussing medication or medical treatment with doctors, advising on suitable clothing or activities. In most situations, professionals dealing with someone with profound intellectual and multiple disabilities will be only too glad to be able to talk to someone who is knowledgeable about them. Problems may arise when there is a disagreement, perhaps about standards of care; but parents of adults with learning disabilities have these problems to deal with too, and advice could be sought from MENCAP, the local Community Health Council, and so forth. The present legal situation leaves people with severe learning disabilities in a kind of limbo. New laws are urgently needed to resolve this.

3. There are visiting services for people in residential accommodation – these are organised by voluntary organisations or sometimes by the hospital or residential unit. Someone visits the disabled person regularly, befriends them and takes a long-term interest in their welfare. The MENCAP Trustee Visitors' Service is one example. Contact MENCAP for more information. There are other addresses at the end of the chapter.

4. Advocates help to interpret the wishes and best interests of a disabled person, and speak out for them if they cannot do this themselves. They are often appointed by voluntary organisations, and may in practice befriend and take a general interest in the disabled person. However, the emphasis will be more on advice and ensuring needs and rights are met. (Addresses for information at the end of the chapter.)

5. Appointees and agents are people who manage the day to day financial affairs of someone who cannot do it themselves. When a person with profound intellectual and multiple disabilities reaches the age of 18, their parents or those caring for them will apply to become the appointee, so that they can collect benefits, manage bank and building society accounts, and so on. If the disabled person cannot physically collect the benefits the appointee will also become the agent. If parents die and the disabled person is in residential accommodation, a member of staff will usually become the appointee and/or agent. However, this does not have to be so; if you would like a friend or relative to do this in the event of your death, you can talk to them about it and make a note in your will. This may be particularly important if the disabled person is in or is likely to go to a long-stay hospital, where staff may find it difficult to use money in their account for their personal benefit.

FUNERAL ARRANGEMENTS

You may not want to think about this. But if you were no longer alive, and your son or daughter with profound intellectual and multiple disabilities died, someone would have to decide on these arrangements. It is not easy to interpret the beliefs and wishes of someone with this degree of disability. However, if there is a strong family religious and/or cultural tradition, you may wish to ensure that funeral arrangements are carried out in accordance with this. If you have no religious beliefs, it is possible for a ceremony to be carried out which reflects the interests and achievements of the person who has died, with music they enjoyed.

When Kathy died, we realised how important it was for us, her relatives and many friends and carers, to express our love and to remember the achievements of her life, and to say farewell to her together. We realised that the ceremony was particularly important for her friends with learning disabilities who were having to try to understand her death. We chose music she loved and a friend played the flute. Friends who knew and loved her spoke. Good friends helped us to plan this, and then made the practical arrangements for us. Despite our great sorrow at her death, we were helped to be proud of her and her life.

There are some practical things you can do to make sure that things are carried out as you would wish:

1. Make a note of the exact arrangements for the funeral – where, religious service or not, choice of music, who will speak, flowers or not, and anything else that is important to you. Leave a copy of this with your will. Make sure that copies are left with those who will be responsible for the person you care for if you die. You may like to make sure that close relatives have a copy.

2. You can take out a pre-payment plan to cover funeral expenses. There are several; contact Age Concern to ask for details. (You can take out one of these plans at any age.) It means you can decide on things like cremation or burial, type of coffin, and the general style of the arrangements, beforehand. When someone you love has just died, it can be heartbreaking to have to discuss such practical details. It also means that there is no worry about meeting expenses at the time. You can pay by various methods including instalments. The price you are offered is guaranteed.

I DON'T WANT TO KNOW ABOUT ANY OF THIS

This is your choice. It is very painful to think of any of the matters covered in this chapter. However, you have devoted your life to caring for someone with profound intellectual and multiple disabilities. You would not let them down knowingly. If you are no longer able to care, or even there at all, someone else will make any necessary decisions. You can have some effect on those decisions, and therefore on the future life of the person you have cared for, by planning ahead in the ways suggested.

FURTHER INFORMATION

Age Concern England, Astral House, 1268 London Road, London SW16 4ER. Tel: 081–679–8000. Advice about pre-paid funeral plans. You may have a local Age Concern who can advise.

Citizen Advocacy, Unit 2K, Leroy House, 436 Essex Road, London N1 3QP. Tel: 071–359–8289. Information about schemes where trained volunteers represent the interests, rights and needs of someone with a learning disability.

Court of Protection, Enquiries: 071–269–7000. Information booklets.

MENCAP, The Royal Society for Mentally Handicapped Children and Adults, 123, Golden Lane, London EC1Y ORT. Tel: 071–454–0454, for information about:

> The Adcare Foundation
>
> The Mencap Trustee Visitors Service
>
> National Trustees for the Mentally Handicapped Limited
>
> Information pack on leaving money and property to people with learning disabilities.

Network for the Handicapped, 16 Princeton Street, London WC1R 4BB. Tel: 071–831–8031/7740. Legal advice.

Publications

After I'm Gone, What will happen to my Handicapped Child? by Gerald Sanctuary. Souvenir Press, Human Horizons Series, ISBN 0–285–65092–0.

Mental Handicap and the Law by Gordon Ashton. Sweet and Maxwell. ISBN: 0 421 42000 6.

Part Seven

Conclusion

Conclusion

WHO CARES FOR THE CARERS?

This book has been about getting the best possible deal for the disabled person you care for. But the carers must also have their needs considered. You need to make sure the person with the disabilities has had the best attention possible. Physiotherapy, for example, may make all the difference between someone becoming twisted and uncomfortable, or remaining able to sit, eat and take part in what is going on. But you also need to make sure you and other members of the family are not exhausted and drained by hospital visiting, anxiety, missing meals, lack of rest and recreation.

Those of us who care for anyone with a chronic condition, where episodes can occur at any hour or on any day, are soon forced to learn to live with the decisions we regularly have to make and often to rehearse potential happenings that go with those decisions. Apart from the conditions from which someone may be suffering, and which may need decisions about how and when and where to, there are things like the possibility of accidental fractures, for example, which can happen to anyone but present particular problems for someone who is frail, with fragile bones and less able to withstand general anaesthesia. We find ourselves thinking ahead, not in any really pessimistic mood but because it is part of our lives to know that quite grave problems may arise and corresponding decisions be made.

Should you give this new medication a try? What about possible side effects? What about this operation – what are the dangers, how might it improve things; is it worth the risk? Shall we save to buy a private wheelchair, hearing or communications aids, because the NHS provision is not good enough? What about residential school – can it offer the best chances, how will we all cope with the separation? Shall I give up work? Should I get a job? Shall I go to the papers about this problem that the services have failed to deal with? Should we move house to be near specialist facilities? Shall I leave my family and stay in hospital with my disabled daughter or son – maybe over and over again? Shall I tell the grandparents the full extent of the problem? Can I tell my partner how anxious and distressed I feel? Should we phone for the ambulance now? Would it be quicker to take her to casualty by car; can we risk it?

One of the most difficult decisions is undoubtedly over whether to use respite care or long term residential facilities. No one else can make this decision for you. You can ask for advice and opinions, especially from people who have faced the same problems. But your health, energy levels, emotional resilience and family circumstances are unique to you. Often you can judge for yourself whether you are coping or not. Sometimes you need other people to tell you that you and your partner are always snapping at each other, that other children feel neglected, that you look ill or tired or both, that you seem to be overwhelmed by the many demands on you.

If this is you, no one else has the right to make you feel guilty for seeking some relief. Regular, reliable respite care would help to prevent some of these problems threatening the well-being of you and the family.

Residential school for the under-eighteens may serve two purposes. It may provide better opportunities for development of skills than local schools. It also gives the family a break from constant caring. You will still need to face up to what happens when your disabled daughter or son reaches school-leaving age.

Residential care is a more permanent option and therefore involves a much more difficult decision. You have to balance everyone's needs. Some of us take up this option when the person with the disabilities is comparatively young. We would not have done it if we felt there was any other way. It is heartbreaking to give your child into the hands of strangers; many of us have said it is like a bereavement. This decision is easier if the residential facility is local, and you can drop in and out and share the care. You are more likely to feel bad about it if the unit is a long distance away, if travelling difficulties make visiting hard and if you do not feel involved in the care.

With adults, leaving the parental home for another residential setting should be seen as a natural stage in the life of anyone, however severe their disabilities. The greatest fear of most parents and carers is about what will happen when they are not able to go on caring through incapacity or death. This fear can never be entirely removed, but it will help if you can plan ahead long before this is likely to happen. You can then take part in the planning of future arrangements and can involve the person you care for in seeing the move as a positive one. I have discussed this issue in more detail in Chapters 11, 12 and 22.

It is a joy shared with whoever is cared for to engage in all the things that can be done together, but at the happiest times you are aware that a crisis may suddenly occur. A phone call when the person you care for is at school or centre, or being cared for elsewhere, is almost expected to bring bad news. It does become a part of life to be apprehensive at times as well as positive and well-organised, and it is because of this that the support of families with similar experiences is more valuable than just sharing hints and tips and practicalities.

It also means that it is a very difficult thing for many without this experience to grasp fully what it constantly entails. Even with all the physical and organisational support, and in those periods where all goes smoothly and happily and a holiday is just around the corner, it is an experience apart and one which relatively few will come to share. Maybe different friends who have shared that experience will find different words which explain it for them, and the dimensions of responsibility for care and feelings as a parent are different too, but there is and there remains a gravity in life. If you can live with this and still make the best of life's good moments, you will do more than just survive.

Index